ON MY WAY HOME

365 DEVOTIONAL POEMS

Jane Spears

On My Way Home

© Copyright 2024 Jane Spears
ISBN: 978-1-951602-31-4

Unless otherwise noted, all scriptures are taken from The Holy Bible, New International Version®, copyright © 1973, 1978, 1984, 2011 by Biblical, Inc.tm Used by permission of Zondervan. All rights reserved worldwide. www.zondervan.com.

Scripture marked AKJV refers to the Authorized King James Version, which is the pure Cambridge edition (1901). Public Domain

Scriptures marked AMP are taken from the AMPLIFIED® BIBLE, Copyright © 1954, 1958, 1962, 1964, 1965, 1987 by the Lockman Foundation Used by Permission. (www.Lockman.org).

Scriptures marked are taken from the Holy Bible: Easy-to-Read Version (ERV), International Edition © 2013, 2016 by Bible League International and used by permission.

Scriptures marked ESV are from The Holy Bible, English Standard Version® (ESV®), copyright © 2001 by Crossway, a publishing ministry of Good News Publishers. Used by permission. All rights reserved.

Scriptures marked KJV are from The Holy Bible, the Authorized (King James) Version.

Scriptures marked MSG are taken from the THE MESSAGE: THE BIBLE IN CONTEMPORARY ENGLISH: copyright©1993, 1994, 1995, 1996, 2000, 2001, 2002. Used by permission of NavPress Publishing Group.

Scriptures marked NLT are taken from the HOLY BIBLE, NEW LIVING TRANSLATION, Copyright© 1996, 2004, 2007 by Tyndale House Foundation. Used by permission of Tyndale House Publishers, Inc., Carol Stream, Illinois 60188. All rights reserved. Used by permission.

Scriptures marked NKJV are from The Holy Bible, the New King James Version®. Copyright © 1982 by Thomas Nelson. Used by permission. All rights reserved.

Scripture quotations marked TPT are from The Passion Translation®. Copyright © 2017, 2018, 2020 by Passion & Fire Ministries, Inc. Used by permission. All rights reserved. ThePassionTranslation.com.

All rights reserved. No part of this publication may be reproduced or transmitted in any form or by any means without written permission from the publisher.

Cover designed by my daughter, Holly Reid

Published by:
Faith-Driven Books, an imprint of Write Integrity Press
PO Box 702852; Dallas, TX 75370
www.WriteIntegrity.com

Published in the United States of America.

Dedication

Lovingly dedicated to Dad and Mom

Dad, thank you for the immediacy of your answer
to the sincerity of my question of knowing about eternal life.
You opened the Bible and read to my listening ears the assurance
found in 1 John 5:13 that states, *I write these things to you who
believe in the Name of the Son of God
so that you may know that you have eternal life.*
That moment is a forever treasured memory.

And Mom, thank you for redirecting my heart to the Word
when my heart was beyond broken. You knew that I could only
find healing and comfort through the Lord healing my heart.
And later on down the road, you told me you believed that I
would someday be writing a devotional…
and that someday has come.

Thank you both for making certain I would eternally know
the way Home…

*So then faith comes by hearing, and hearing by the Word of God.
Romans 10:17*

Table of Contents

Dedication 5
Foreword 7
Introduction 8
January 9
February 51
March 83
April 125
May 161
June 199
July 241
August 275
September 307
October 341
November 377
December 411
About the Author 453

Foreword

What in this day do You want me to hear
Peace be still for I am near
What in this day do You want me to see
All of you is held by Me

What in this day do You want me to say
Yes to trusting My unending ways
What in this day do You want me to know
The Grace of Calvary's forgiving flow

*O Lord my God, I called to You
for help and You healed me.
Psalm 30:2*

Then sings my soul…

Introduction

We have an appointment to keep
As You awaken my soul from sweet sleep
Moving my heart then my feet
Within Your faithfulness there to meet

Morning mercies given each day
Refreshing moments Your gracious way
To come seek and truly find
Rest inside my heart my mind

Continuously You supply
All that is needed to rely
Upon this kinship given throughout time
For my heart to know You as mine

Give thanks to the Lord for He is good;
His love endures forever.
Psalm 118:1

The Lord appeared to us in the past, saying,
"I have loved you with an everlasting love;
I have drawn you with unfailing kindness."
Jeremiah 31:3 NIV

JANUARY

January 1
Adam and his wife were both naked,
and they felt no shame.
Genesis 2:25

The innocence in the garden before the snake
The innocence in the garden before they chose to forsake
The innocence they knew until suddenly introduced to shame
The innocence now hidden within layers of blame

The innocence not cherished but rejected
The innocence once known but not selected
The innocence given to dwell forever within
The innocence destroyed by the surrender to sin

The innocence of mankind was wholly restored
The innocence resurrected by Jesus Christ as Lord
The innocence cherished and surrendered unto
The innocence mended through the miracle of You

A record of the genealogy of Jesus Christ
the son of David, the son of Abraham.
Matthew 1:1

Hopelessness in the Genesis of two
Hopefulness in Matthew's news of You…

January 2

You are more than a house or cupboard can hold
You are more precious than the wisemen's gold
You are uncontainable indescribable
You are poetically undefinable

And yet You house and fill my soul
With endless joy sent to overflow
A spillway from Heaven touching the earth
Before the beginning and Giver of worth

You are my journal entry each day
In the words You poetically say
Demonstrating graciously to my soul
Your spillway of Heaven given to know…

Thanks be to God for His indescribable Gift.
2 Corinthians 9:15

January 3
*I lie down and sleep; I wake again,
because the Lord sustains me.
Psalm 3:5*

If there were no words to write
You would still be there throughout the night
If there were no words to say
You would still be there without delay

If there were no sight to see
You would still be there beyond degree
If there were no sound to hear
You would still be there tenderly near

If there were no rhythm or rhyme
You would still be there all through time
If there were no ripple effects
You would still be there to gladly connect

If there were no wind for the sail
You would still be there without fail
If there were no pearls in a shell
You would still be there as Emmanuel

*If I go up to the heavens, You are there;
if I make my bed in the depths; You are there.
If I rise on the wings of the dawn,
if I settle on the far side of the sea,
even there Your Hand will guide me,
Your right Hand will hold me fast.
Psalm 139:8-10*

January 4

Daily You send Your miracle of light
That puts an end to the darkness of night
Daily You speak to unsettled feet
Gently supplying Your Peace and Your Strength

Daily You show each heart each soul
Mercy as warm as a sunrise glow
Daily You still embedded clay
Rooted in Your groundbreaking ways

Daily You shelter as You reign
Leaving our hearts forever changed
Daily You see your kingdom won
Foreshadowed Grace Your forever outcome

...the people living in darkness have seen a great light;
on those living in the land of the shadow of death
a light has dawned.
Matthew 4:16

January 5

What a miracle to have Your Word
And read exactly what was heard
Thank You for the time it took
To have Your Story in a book

Oh the timeless gift to hold
Every sentence that unfolds
Your love letter for every soul
Handwritten for the world to know

*I would like to learn just one thing from you:
Did you receive the Spirit by the works of the law,
or by believing what you heard?
Galatians 3:2*

*So again I ask, does God give you His Spirit and
work miracles among you by the works of the law,
or by believing what you heard?
Galatians 3:5*

On My Way Home

Tell me the story of Jesus,
Write on my heart every word;
Tell me the story most precious,
Sweetest that ever was heard…
-Fanny Crosby, 1880

…by believing what you heard…

What a miracle to have Your Word
And read exactly what was heard
Thank You for the time it took
To have Your Story in a book…

January 6

For we brought nothing into the world,
and we can take nothing out of it.
1 Timothy 6:7

As we sift through our stuff of earth
Memories made through trials that hurt
Revisiting moments not meant to stay
Deciding what to keep and throw away

Even as we release what once was held
Our life experiences are memories not shelved
The ebb and flow in the river of life
Has shaped and transformed us as husband and wife

The letting go and holding on
Takes on new meaning every dawn
There's more ahead than behind
Life lessons learned throughout time

Pressing on and leaning into
Unseen Footprints leading through
Precisely where into our now
Hand in hand as He allows

The Grace of "through" that teaches much
Has been the glue that tendered us
There were no steps without His Hand
Holding ours through hour-glassed sand

January 7
Teach us to be still enough among the motion
Quiet us longingly by Your devotion
Instill us to listen and longingly respond
To Your entrusted promptings our lifelong

Teach us that stillness is a gift
That You longingly never dismiss
Quiet us intentionally each day
To longingly receive the words You say

A longing fulfilled is sweet to the soul.
Proverbs 13:19

January 8

Appointed for eyes to daily know
Anointed beauty from His Heart aglow
In the sunrise across the sky
Symbolizing faithfulness His Heart nearby

Intentional rocks there to see
A heartfelt message formed perfectly
Rock of Ages cleft for me
Firm foundation unshakably

Everlasting Heart hung on that tree
Given to purify sacredly
Washing away what we could not carry
Came to once and for all forgive and bury

All placed upon His willing Heart
To finalize redemption's part
Freely given then and each day
His Heart was formed to give away

And as we fall unmistakably
Upon His Grace undeniably
His Heart transforms ours throughout time
Rock of Ages' hallowed design…

*He is the Rock, His works are perfect, and all His ways are just.
A faithful God who does no wrong, upright and just is He.
Deuteronomy 32:4*

>Rock of Ages, cleft for me,
>Let me hide myself in Thee;
>Let the water and the blood,
>From Thy wounded side which flowed,
>Be of sin the double cure,
>Save from wrath and make me pure.
>-Augustus M. Toplady, 1776

January 9

Isaac spoke up and said to his father Abraham, "Father?"
"Yes, my son?" Abraham replied.
"The fire and the wood are here," Isaac said, "but where is the lamb for the burnt offering?"
Abraham answered, "God Himself will provide the lamb for the burnt offering, my son." And the two of them went on together."
Genesis 22:7-8

The Lord will provide
His promise to guide
His Grace and merciful ways
Throughout our lives every day

Abraham believed the first words
That God spoke and he heard
That is how he was able to go
Up the mountain with the son he loved so

God watched from on high
Willingness of Abraham to let his son die
But that was not that day's plan
He had in a thicket a substitute ram

Someday soon God would see
His One and Only die at Calvary
He always knew this day would come
When He would give up His Only Son

He also knew beyond that day
The appointed miracle beyond the grave
Through the willingness He alone gave
Would be the only way for us to be saved

*So Abraham called that place The Lord Will Provide.
And to this day it is said, "On this mountain of
the Lord it will be provided."
Genesis 22:14*

Come Thou Fount of every blessing
Tune my heart to sing Thy Grace
Streams of mercy never ceasing
Calls for songs of loudest praise
-Robert Robinson, 1758

*I will give thanks to You, Lord, with all of my heart;
I will tell of all Your wonderful deeds.
I will be glad and rejoice in You;
I will sing the praises of Your Name, O Most High.
Psalm 9:1-2*

January 10
Be astonished and wait
His timing is never late
Be astonished and see
His answer affirmatively

Be astonished and hear
His Word He brings near
Be astonished and believe
His provision for each need

Be astonished and bring
Awe to His wellspring
Be astonished and behold
His anointed blessings tenfold

*Let love and faithfulness never leave you;
bind them around your neck, write them on
the tablet of your heart.
Trust in the Lord with all your heart and lean not
on your own understanding; in all your ways
acknowledge Him and He will make your paths straight.
Proverbs 3:3, 5-6*

January 11

Be still and know
[recognize and understand] that I am God.
I will be exalted among the nations!
I will be exalted in the earth.
Psalm 46:10 AMP

Recognize My footnotes of Grace
Recognize My noted pace
Recognize the image I bear
Recognize I am aware

Recognize My righteousness
Recognize My greatest quest
Recognize My mercies new
Recognize My love for you

January 12

Isaac couldn't see but his wife could still hear
Eavesdropping with her listening ear
To the instructions from father to son
Rebekah's overhearing eventually put Jacob on the run

But before the haste of flight
She made sure Jacob had Isaac's blessing for life
Using deception she instructed Jacob to lie
To go to his father pretending the eldest had supplied

Isaac trusted his sense of taste touch and smell
Ignoring the sound of the voice he knew well
Asking exactly if his name was Esau
What was Jacob thinking hairy patches and all

The takeaway was more than Esau could bear
Losing both his firstborn shares
In sorrow he wept for what was stolen
Heart with Cain-rage invoked and swollen

Jacob's takeaway was more than could be carried
Told to leave or he would be buried
Left in haste from his deceitful pact
With his burden no looking back
(Inspired by *Genesis 27*)

January 13

The Lord appeared to us in the past, saying:
"I have loved you with an everlasting love;
I have drawn you with unfailing kindness."
Jeremiah 31:3

To my Savior I am drawn
In the quiet every dawn
Drawn to experience once again
Gracious goodness without end

To my Savior I am drawn
In the quiet to come along
Drawn to His gentleness conveyed
Leading in His resurrected Way

To my Savior I am drawn In the quiet every dawn
Drawn to read His Word given
Receiving His message purpose driven

To my Savior I am drawn In the quiet to come along
Drawn to pastures green prepared
Newfound mercies awaiting there

"…I have drawn you…with unfailing kindness."
Jeremiah 31:3

Beautiful Savior! Lord of the nations!
Son of God and Son of man!
Glory and honor, Praise, adoration,
Now and forevermore be Thine!
-Fairest Lord Jesus
Anonymous, 1677

January 14

Every today was yesterday's tomorrow
Every heartache known before it owned sorrow
No thought or step will there ever be
That is not Graced in God's Sovereignty

The protective Hand that leads
Knows every inseparable need
That our hearts will experience and know
And that is why our Shepherd won't let go

He directs the wayward sheep
He recognizes every bleat
He rescues and endlessly redeems
He lovingly cherishes through His Blood as the means

Sustaining through what devastates us
Mending brokenness through His tenderness
Teaching through whatever is faced
That He is unrivaled unending Grace

On My Way Home

He Shepherds and willingly sustains
Through the power of His Name
Nothing can come or even collide
Without pure Mercy He provides

Thank You that You bring hearts through
All the heartache we wouldn't choose
And You unendingly graciously hold
The sustaining relief You desire all to know

Surely God is my Help; The Lord is the One Who sustains me.
Psalm 54:4

January 15
When hard pressed, I cried to the Lord; He brought me into a
spacious place. The Lord is with me; I will not be afraid.
What can mere mortals do to me?
Psalm 118:5

Wrestling through the promise Jacob had heard
Praying protection from his brother's angry words
Quenching one fire from where he had just departed
Now facing his initial reason for being downhearted

Jacob, like us, knew what he deserved
Longing to live and be reassured
Crying out in fear he prayed
And found like us Your faithful ways

There is no matter too small or great
There is no reason to not articulate
Whatever is hanging over our heads
Seeking Your guidance to be directed and led

You know the way each footprint will go
You have the timeline that You willingly show
You wait for obedient steps to comply
You have such patience for Jacob…and I…

Thank You for Your quieting in my soul
That through You alone I can rest and know
Love that not only answers and surrounds
But new mercies that continually astound

And the Peace of God, which transcends all understanding,
will guard your hearts and minds in Christ Jesus.
Philippians 4:7

My faith has found a resting place…
-Lidie H. Edmunds, 1891

January 16
Jacob, now Israel, sent a message ahead
To greet Esau's heart where their feet were led
Showing his willingness to make amends
Knowing this meeting on forgiveness depends

John the Baptist, the messenger, was sent ahead
The meeting for all hearts to be Shepherd led
Sharing the message that makes forever amends
Knowing this meeting on forgiveness depends

Oh, that salvation for Israel would come out of Zion!
When the Lord restores His people,
let Jacob rejoice and Israel be glad!
Psalm 14:7

For it is by Grace you have been saved,
through faith and this is not from yourselves,
it is the gift of God
Ephesians 2:8

January 17
When there are no words to say
You are still holding me through each day
When I cannot even think
You are still holding me in Your Strength

When I stumble on my way
You are still holding me fast always
When I walk through the unknown
You are still holding me I'm never alone

*And the Peace of God, which transcends
all understanding, will guard your
hearts and minds in Christ Jesus.
Philippians 4:7*

I hear the Savior say,
"Thy strength indeed is small
Child of weakness watch and pray
Find in Me thine all in all."
-Elvina M. Hall, 1865

January 18
Trust like Joseph in his dreams
Trust no matter the confusing scenes
Trust like lives depend on it
Trust that God is using this

Trust that He will never leave
Trust He knows the moments we grieve
Trust the famine as part of the plan
Trust the roadmap in His Hand

Trust the eyes that sees each need
Trust the timing and believe
Trust the outcome He already knows
Trust His comfort He foretold

What our hearts would not know
If not for the intermission of sorrow…
What our hearts would not see
If not for Mercy undeservingly…

On My Way Home

*But the wisdom that comes from heaven
is first of all pure; then peace-loving,
considerate, submissive, full of mercy and good fruit,
impartial and sincere.*
James 3:17

O Love that will not let me go
I rest my weary soul in Thee
I give Thee back the life I owe
That in Thine ocean depths its flow
May richer, fuller be
-George Matheson, 1865

January 19
There is a rhythm of slowing down
To quiet my soul in solitude found
To attentively listen and hear each day
Finding renewal each step of the way

There is a rhythm that You reveal
Answering the invitation to be intentionally still
Opening up the tight-fisted palm
Exchanging my ways for Your calm

There is a rhythm I desire to know
Every moment deep in my soul
That lands completely at Your Feet
As the Grace I'm given to repeat

There is a rhythm of longing within
That only You can heal and deepen
Reflecting the season and its pace
Held each step in Your embrace

*You will seek Me and find Me
when you seek Me with all your heart.
Jeremiah 29:13*

January 20
I am with you, declares the Lord.
Haggai 1:13

With you always every single day
With you always in every single way
With you always when darkness pervades
With you always is My promise I have made

With you always for you through all time
With you always for you are chosen as Mine
With you always no matter what you face
With you always holding in My Comfort and Grace

And surely I am with you always,
to the very end of the age.
Matthew 28:20

January 21
For all have sinned and fall short of the glory of God,
and all are justified freely
by His Grace through the redemption that came by Christ Jesus.
Romans 3:23-24

Forgiveness is our greatest need
God gave Jesus for our debt and deeds
No greater Love would willingly die
For every sin for our very lives

Incongruent our sin cast on Him
And our gift is to live forgiven
Thank You for the Grace of Grace
That You allow in unending pace…

Because of YOU alone
"It Is Well" is fully known
Because of Your forgiveness
"It Is Well" inside us

My sin, O the bliss of this glorious thought
My sin, not in part but the whole
Is nailed to the Cross, and I bear it no more
Praise the Lord, praise the Lord, O my soul
It is well…with my soul…
-Horatio G. Spafford, 1873

On My Way Home

Praying now His comfort and peace
That can never ever cease
He knows and sees every part
Of the brokenness in each heart

He gave His Life that wholly mends
That brings cleansing healing deep within
Through forgiveness that we not only know
But in turn can give to other broken souls

Fill my heart, Jesus, with only You
So I can breathe and walk anew
In the realm of such merciful Grace
Through the Sinless One that took my place

For God so loved the world that He gave…
John 3:16

January 22

When Pharaoh calls you in and asks,
"What is your occupation?" you should answer,
"Your servants have tended livestock from our boyhood on,
just as our fathers did."
Then you will be allowed to settle in the region
of Goshen, for all shepherds are detestable to the Egyptians.
Genesis 46:33-34

Detestable played a role of distinct
Drawing a line of protection and length
Between Egypt and Goshen as God's plan
Where Jacob brought his family from the Promised Land

Settling far enough away
As shepherds for their 430 year stay
Before the enslavement ever took place
Before the Passover Lamb of Grace…

Shepherds played an intricate part
Of the Christmas Story known by heart
First to arrive to see God's Passover Lamb
Who brought forever freedom His shepherding plan

I am the Good Shepherd.
John 10:14

January 23

The law of the Lord is perfect reviving the soul.
The statutes of the Lord are trustworthy, making wise the simple.
The precepts of the Lord are right giving joy to the heart.
The commands of the Lord are radiant giving light to the eyes.
The fear of the Lord is pure, enduring forever.
The ordinances of the Lord are sure and altogether righteous.
Psalm 19:7-9

You alone revive my soul
You alone quiet to be still and know
You alone give wisdom to grow
You alone entrust and peace bestow

You alone infuse my heart
You alone are joy that never departs
You alone are the radiant Light
You alone are the breath of delight

You alone are purity without measure
You alone are forever found Treasure
You alone are the foundation of sure
You alone are the Rock secure

The Lord is my Rock…
Psalm 18:2

My Hope is built on nothing less
Than Jesus blood and righteousness
I dare not trust the sweetest frame
But WHOLLY lean on Jesus Name

On Christ the solid Rock I stand
All other ground is sinking sand
-Edward Mote, 1834

January 24

When Jacob had finished giving instructions to his sons,
he drew his feet up into the bed,
breathed his last and was gathered to his people.
Genesis 49:33

Another era had passed away
The goodbyes to his sons that day
The blessings given to each one
Spoken to rest upon each son

Then he drew his last breath
Eyes closing in death
No more deceit as in his given name
But to be remembered as one being changed

No longer Jacob but Israel after wrestling in the night
Limping away for the rest of his life
Having heartache at his end redeemed
Teaches us faithfulness graces every life scene

May the Lord answer you when you are in distress;
may the Name of the God of Jacob protect you.
Psalm 20:1

As Jacob wrestled so do we
As Jacob wondered so do we
As Jacob ran so do we
As Jacob feared so do we

As I read Your Word tears come
Awed by Your faithfulness to everyone
There is no realm of impossible with You
Grace and Mercy make all things new

You have set times in delays
To grow in trust in Your ways
Teaching nothing is impossible for You
That intentional timing is what You use

Waiting timed like seed to flower
To see the bloom at its appointed hour
Time was created within each day
To see Your faithfulness on its way

Yet God has made everything beautiful for its time. He has planted eternity in the human heart, but even so, people cannot see the whole scope of God's work from beginning to end.
Ecclesiastes 3:11, NLT

January 25

But when she could hide him no longer,
she got a papyrus basket for him and coated it with tar and pitch.
Then she placed the child in it and put it among the reeds
along the bank of the Nile.
His sister stood at a distance to see what would happen to him.
Exodus 2:3-4

The sacrifice Moses' Mother made
That day in a basket her baby laid
Entrusting him into the Hands that made hers
Sending Miriam to watch and observe

Just like the casting of bread on the water
So she received the news from her daughter
The permission granted to nurse her child
That had been placed in the river Nile

Amazing to hold her baby again
Out of danger protected from men
The giving away was trusting faith
The receiving back was amazing grace

January 26
Thank You for closets that hold Your keepsakes
Thank You for Grace that's never timed late
Thank You for the protective Shelter of prayer
Thank You that no storm separates from Your watch care

Thank You for the permanence of You
Thank You for the storms you bring us through
Thank You for Your promise of steadfastness
Thank You for the grandeur of Your unendingness

Thank You for faith that gives You glory
Thank You for hearts that live out Your Story
Thank You for Your promise to never leave nor forsake
Thank You for closets that hold Your keepsakes

...even there Your Hand will guide me,
Your right Hand will hold me fast.
Psalm 139:10

(Dedicated to friends that were protected in their closet during a tornado losing their home but not their faith...)

January 27
Pharaoh's dream was God's merciful plan
To give abundance before the famine
To let the nation for seven years prepare
For what was ahead and to live aware

This was all inclusive for everyone's need
Provision supplied abundantly to feed
It was a "lack" to move Jacob to come
Into the "dream" of Joseph his son

Not a dream was wasted then
That God had purposed timed and given
Piecing the puzzle together over time
Exactly the way God had designed

Joseph's heartache was not in vain
God's perfect timing was prearranged
To restore the family torn apart
By jealousy that pervaded hearts

God's plan was not to end in despair
But to bring the brothers to Egypt with their wares
In exchange to bow and know
Mercy in a way "they" did not show

Joseph had a choice he was in charge
To get revenge greater than large
But God preserved his heart for good
For a family reunion not yet understood

*And all the world came to Egypt to buy grain from Joseph,
because the famine was severe everywhere.
Genesis 41:57*

*Although Joseph recognized his brothers,
they did not recognize him.
Then he remembered his dreams about them…
Genesis 42:8-9*

January 28

Therefore, say to the Israelites: I am the Lord, and
"I will" bring you out from under the yoke of the Egyptians.
"I will" free you from being slaves to them, and
"I will" redeem you with an outstretched arm and with mighty
acts of judgment.
"I will" take you as My own people, and "I will" be your God.
Then you will know that I am the Lord your God, who brought you
out from under the yoke of the Egyptians. And "I will" bring you
to the land I swore with uplifted hand to give to Abraham, to Isaac
and to Jacob. "I will" give it to you as a possession. I am the Lord.
Exodus 6:6-8

The "I will" of God will never fail
The "I will" of God will unendingly prevail
The "I will" of God is for each to embrace
The "I will" of God is His unending pace

The "I will" of God was His purposed plan
The "I will" of God through His outstretched Hand
The "I will" of God goes before and behind
The "I will" of God is for all souls to find

Because the Lord is my Shepherd:
I will lack nothing I will live restored
I will never walk alone I will fear no evil

I will live comforted I will rest in prepared provision
I will walk surrounded in goodness and love
I will dwell in the house of the Lord forever…

Not my will, but Thine be done.
Luke 22:42

January 29
God is within her, she will not fall;
God will help her at break of day.
Psalm 46:5

The constancy of Your Heart to mine
Is beyond gloriously divine
The Word You daily speak to me
Gives my heart its joy and wings

The constancy of Your calm each dawn
Is sweet rest to walk upon
Seamless is Your perfect Peace
That unendingly brings me strength

The constancy of Your unending ways
Is Your Grace and constant stay
Thank You for Your constancy
That You designed to strengthen me

January 30
In famine and without the people came
Surrendering all they had as Pharaoh's claim
But there came the day when things were reversed
And Egypt felt each plague as a curse

The location no longer was the place to be
Hence God led the Israelites out of captivity
Showing His power through His miraculous signs
That was for all to see Pharaoh's change of mind

Intended for the chosen people to go
Three days journey to worship God so
All would know deliverance had come
Just like Moses had told everyone

"Not a hoof is to be left behind
All are clearly to be freed as Mine"
The four hundred years of slavery done
Just like Abraham had told everyone

See the unending connection
Of God's holy perfection
His Story throughout the ages
Housed within His written pages

See the magnitude of His pursuit
Of making certain all hear the Truth
Giving His Word that never passes away
Giving Salvation freely each day

Like the garden still giving the choice
To listen then choose to follow His Voice
Finding the outstretched Hands has supplied
The fruitfulness of forgiveness that changes lives

Touching every other part
Did not touch the hardened heart
Until the firstborn sons died that day
That was the "final straw" of Egypt's stay

Fast forward to a future bed of straw
Where our Savior came for all
To deliver from captivity
God giving His firstborn intentionally

Trust in the Lord forever, for the Lord,
The Lord Himself is the Rock eternal.
Isaiah 26:34

January 31

You are our Grace and remedy
You are our Mercy unendingly
You are our Deliverer and Passover Lamb
You are our Righteousness and Great I AM

You are our Holiness living inside
You are our Hope that forever abides
You are our Provider of every breath
You are our Shepherd leading each step

*I am with you and will watch
over you wherever you go.
Genesis 28:15*

FEBRUARY

February 1

*Moses took the bones of Joseph with him because
Joseph had made the Israelites swear an oath.
He had said, "God will surely come to your aid, and then
you must carry my bones up with you from this place."
Exodus 13:19*

Israel carried a promise within
Spoken by Joseph to each of them
A time would come that they would leave
Egypt's land that had provided their need

We carry a promise deep within
Spoken by Jesus to followers of Him
A time will come when we will leave
This place provided we will no longer need

We carry the Spirit now within
Spoken clearly to fishers of men
A time given before each of us leave
To share His Provision that we all need

February 2
First in the desert the Living Water
Sustaining there every son and daughter
Then the raining down of Bread
Foreshadowing of the Good Shepherd ahead

All the desert needs He supplied
Attentive to their every cry
Teaching through the wilderness
How to trust His faithfulness

Oh the lessons there applied
Within the desert of our lives
Shepherding sustaining supplying always
Unendingly miraculously throughout all our days

So where You lead will I go
Will I trust You with all my soul
Help me to listen daily and cling
To Your gracious Shepherding

Look to the Lord and His Strength;
Seek His Face always.
Psalm 105:4

February 3
You are the God Who sees me.
Genesis 16:13

You are the God Who sees
Every part of me
You are the God Who knows
Every part of my soul

You are the God Who hears
Every part of my fears
You are the God Who calms
Every part of my qualms

You are the God Who engages
Every part of my life stages
You are the God Who saves
Every part of my name engraved

You are the God Who deepens
Every part of my heart strengthens
You are the God Who restores
Every part of my heart forevermore

February 4
No matter if I am up or down
Your Song is the unending sound
No matter if I am coming or going
Your Heart teaches mine the gift of slowing

No matter if I am busy or not
Your Faithfulness does not ever stop
No matter if I am noisy or quiet
Your Grace is never on hold or silent

No matter if I go or stay
Your Word remains forever always
No matter if I am rushed or delayed
Your morning mercies are what matter each day

The Lord bless you and keep you;
the Lord make His face shine upon you
and be gracious to you;
the Lord turn His face toward you and give you peace.
Numbers 6:24-26

February 5
Acronym for DIFFICULTIES

Demonstration of
Immanuel's
Faithful
Footprints
In
Circumstances
Under-
Lining
The
Impossible
Echoing
Sufficiency

*But He said to me, "My grace is sufficient for you,
for My power is made perfect in weakness."
2 Corinthians 12:9*

February 6
You fill the emptiness with Your Grace
You fill the loneliness with Your embrace
You fill the tiredness with Your quieted Rest
You fill the hopelessness with Your effortless best

*See I am sending an angel ahead of you to guard you along
the way and to bring you to the place I have prepared for you.
Exodus 23:20*

God is guarding you now
Along the way when you don't see how
God is bringing you to the exactness prepared
His answer unfolding to your requested prayer

The activity of God is at work each day
The long part being "along the way" phrase
The timing is happening known step by step
Where every sigh is lovingly kept

Do not lose heart, beloved daughter, today
His faithfulness is never on hold or delay
This part of the journey that's harder than long
Is when He will fill You with His unending Song

*And I will give her her vineyards from there,
and the door of trouble for a door of hope:
and she shall sing THERE.
Hosea 2:15 NKJV*

O Love that wilt not let me go...
-George Matheson, 1882

February 7
Help and Hope for each tear stain
Help and Hope are Power of change
Help and Hope continually sustain
Help and Hope graciously ordained

Help and Hope both needs supply
Help and Hope at each sunrise
Help and Hope enfolded within
Help and Hope both mercifully from Him

*I lift up my eyes to the hills –
where does my help come from?
My help comes from the Lord,
the Maker of heaven and earth.
Psalm 121:1-2*

February 8
Aware of this, Jesus said to them, "Why are you bothering this woman? She has done a beautiful thing to Me." When she poured this perfume on My body, she did it to prepare Me for burial. Truly I tell you, wherever this Gospel is preached throughout the world, what she has done will also be told, in memory of her."
Matthew 26:10, 12-13

In memory of her action that did not wait
Unhindered kindness met by debate
Yet boldly she humbly openly came
Honoring the One Who knew her name

For He knew her everything
He was the One that brought her heart change
She could do nothing less than honor one last time
Grace that was given that wholly refines

Help my heart to live aware
Of Your gracious unending care
Open my eyes to wholly see
Your goodness and intentionality

February 9
O how Psalm Seventy-three
Reaches within the depths of me
After holding the hand that once held mine
Then breathing his last one assigned

Soon after came a soul to speak
Your penned words of comfort and peace
In that moment at the heart of this Psalm
Would be Your Breath of life and calm

Thank You for Your written Word
For the hearts that listened and heard
Penning precisely words You said
To guide my heart to be Shepherd led

Yet I am always with you;
You hold me by my right hand.
You guide me with Your counsel,
and afterward You will take me into glory.
Psalm 73:23-24

February 10
When the Lord finished speaking…
Exodus 31:18

While He was still speaking…
Matthew 26:47a

Not "if" but "while" and "when"
God spoke and speaks again
Recorded in the Old and New
Thread of Hope to hold onto

Correlation clearly seen
In His Word given to glean
He is not faraway but near
Desiring each heart to listen and hear

Timelessness to the finite
Limitlessness His intimate delight
Wholeness His completed goal
Faithfulness to hear and know…

Thy Word is a lamp to my feet
and a light unto my path.
Psalm 119:105 KJV

February 11
There is a pattern of working things together for good
No matter the moments that are misunderstood
Consistently fitting pieces in place
Timed precisely by Your purposeful Grace

Even the dark of night You turn
Even there are life lessons to learn
Even if all seems amiss and awry
Even then Your faithfulness is nigh

Sometimes the waiting of time it takes
Is measured increments to wholly make
A solid work and memory
Of just how gracious Your plan can be

*And we know that all that happens to us is working for our good
if we love God and are fitting into His plans.
Romans 8:28 TLB*

February 12
*Now at the feast the governor was accustomed
to releasing to the multitude
one prisoner whom they wished.
And at that time they had a notorious
prisoner called Barabbas.
Pilate said to them, "Whom do you want me to release to you?
Barabbas, or Jesus who is called the Christ?"
Matthew 27:15-17*

Barabbas was the first to receive pardon and Grace
Of Jesus Christ taking his place
Barabbas knew his horrible crimes
He knew he was one that deserved to die

But this is the greatness of freedom God gives
In pardoning the sinner from death to live
Teaching that Mercy could not be bought
But wholly understood by His Son on the Cross

And we like Barabbas deserve the penalty of death
But Jesus reversed the curse of Adam's breath
Sin and death no longer has the hold
Jesus conquered both as was promised and foretold

Praise the Lord for His gracious Gift
For the sacrifice of Jesus that uplifts
Objects of mercy to gather round the Throne
Complete in Jesus forgiven and known

February 13
This is the day your forevermore
Drinking in your heavenly reward
This is the day appointed to see
Jesus Christ personally

This is the day you taught about
Can only imagine your Hallelujah shout
This is the day your musical theme
Reunited with your Eugene

This is the day made to rejoice
Hearing and answering the Savior's voice
This is the day appointed to be
Circled in red permanently

This is the day you will never forget
The entrance into His benefits
This is the day of welcoming Grace
That you walked into Heaven's embrace

This is the day that Lord has made…

Hold us who wait before Thee
Near to the Heart of God
-Cleland McAfee, 1903
(Miss you, Mom)

February 14

*When Jesus spoke again to the people,
He said, "I am the Light of the world.
Whoever follows Me will never walk in darkness,
but will have the Light of Life."
John 8:12*

What the Light has shown
Is that I am forgiven and fully known
What the Light now tells
Is that I am fully loved by Emmanuel

What the Light continually shows
Is that I am one that He fully knows
What the Light unendingly displays
Is that I am fully redeemed now and always

*Out of His fullness we have all received grace
in place of grace already given.
John 1:16*

Now I Belong To Jesus
by Norman J. Clayton, 1942

February 15
*My whole being will exclaim,
"Who is like You, O Lord?"
Psalm 35:10*

With the Breath You give each day
How I want to pour out praise
With the Life You allow
How I want to serve You now

With the Light You shine
How I want to reflect as Thine
With the Strength You extend
How I want to rely and depend

With the Peace You daily speak
How I want to wholly seek
With the Rest You provide
How I want to there abide

*Now to Him who is able to do immeasurably more
than all we ask or imagine, according to
His power that is at work within us, to Him be glory
in the church and in Christ Jesus throughout
all generations, for ever and ever! Amen.
Ephesians 3:20-21*

February 16
*Some men came, bringing to Him a paralyzed man, carried by
four of them. Since they could not get him to Jesus because of the
crowd, they made an opening in the roof above Jesus by digging
through it and then lowered the mat the man was lying on.
When Jesus saw their faith, he said to the paralyzed man,
"Son, your sins are forgiven. But I want you to know that the Son
of Man has authority on earth to forgive sins."
So He said to the man,
"I tell you, get up, take your mat and go home."
He got up, took his mat and walked out in full view of them all.
This amazed everyone and they praised God, saying,
"We have never seen anything like this!"
Mark 2:3-5, 10-12*

The whole town knew his identity
He was not friendless in his reality
But paralyzed he lay day and night
Hopeless no doubt in his disheartened life

Then came a day that changed his forever
The friends believed and carried him like never
Through the streets to the meeting place
But too many others had beat their pace

Undeterred they willingly climbed
Not leaving their beloved friend behind
Carrying him up to lower him down
In front of Jesus they had finally found

On My Way Home

First forgiven then healed that day
He could walk burdened free as he went on his way
What a lesson for all to visually know
That Jesus is the One Who truly makes whole

No more sin to carry around
When the Grace of Jesus is finally found
Burdened free to walk anew
In mercy filled steps as the unending view

*But now in Christ Jesus you who once were far away
have been brought near by the blood of Christ.
Ephesians 2:13*

February 17
Your love, Lord, reaches to the heavens,
Your faithfulness to the skies.
Psalm 36:5

The place I held and sang each day
The priceless miracles You graciously gave
Holding close for just a while
In the timeline of each child

The place no longer meant to hold
Just the memory that time has told
Moments treasured blanketed there
In the rhythm of my rocking chair

Jesus loves me
He will stay…
Close beside me
all the way…
-Anna Warner, 1860

February 18
*Be still before the Lord
and wait patiently for Him;
do not fret…
Psalm 37:7*

You hold the plan
As well as each hand
You appoint the day
And lead in Your perfect ways

You have no alarm to set
There's no detail You'll forget
Your calendar doesn't flip
There's nothing You could possibly miss

You know beginning without end
All in between are moments You tend
You go with behind and before
For all hearts to know Yours forevermore

February 19

Moses slaughtered the ram and took some of its blood and put it on the lobe of Aaron's right ear, on the thumb of his right hand and on the big toe of his right foot.
Leviticus 8:23

For the right ear
To rightly hear God clear
For the right hand
To rightly do God's commands

For the right toe
To rightly follow God's goal
For the right hearts
To rightly be God's set apart

Consecrate yourselves, for tomorrow the Lord will do amazing things among you.
Joshua 3:5

Consecrate me now to Thy service Lord,
By Thy power of Grace divine;
Let my soul look up with a steadfast Hope,
And my will be lost in Thine
-Draw Me Nearer by Fanny Crosby, 1875

February 20
How precious to me are Your thoughts, O God!
How vast is the sum of them! Were I to count
them, they would outnumber the grains of sand.
When I awake I am still with You.
Psalm 139:17-18

Your thoughts limitless like the sky
Your depths like the ocean that never runs dry
Your counting infinite the only way to describe
Your Presence within You chose to provide

Your thoughts how vast is the sum
Your depths within leaves me undone
Your counting like blessings named one by one
Your Presence within before each day has begun

Thank You for yesterday and for today
Thank You that You are with me now and always
Thank You that nothing can separate me from You
Thank You for Your faithfulness in all that You do

February 21

He pleaded earnestly with Him, "My little daughter is dying. Please come and put Your hands on her so that she will be healed and live." So Jesus went with him. A large crowd followed and pressed around Him. And a woman was there who had been subject to bleeding for twelve years. When she heard about Jesus, she came up behind Him in the crowd and touched His cloak, because she thought, "If I just touch His clothes, I will be healed." Immediately her bleeding stopped and she felt in her body that she was freed from her suffering.
Mark 5:23-25, 27-29

Interruption was not what it seemed
But a testimony to what both of them dreamed
Power of Jesus goes against the norm
He is the Peace for every storm

Interruption to heal thus within
Did not deter Jesus for the request given Him
The healing touch of the hand that reached out
Was for Jairus as well as to believe without doubt

Interruption in the time delayed
Sealed and changed two stories that day
Both waiting desperately for Jesus
His steps always toward in tenderness
Interruption allows more to the story
Timed exact giving greater glory
Perhaps the lesson is to rethink delays
And see more than we could any other way

Rest in the Lord, and wait patiently for Him.
Psalm 37:7 KJV

February 22
Countless blessings will not cease
From Your Heart and Mercyseat
Where we hear Life You speak
From Your Word at Your Feet

More is a word unexplained
More is an adjective of beautiful change
More is a verb of action unending
More is a noun of Shepherd tending

More is the promise that will not cease
More is the Spirit that continually speaks
More is written within each day
More is found from Your Heart always

Alone in the garden wherein is more dew
Alone in the moment where You speak and renew
Alone in the quiet You settle within
Alone in the stillness surrendering begins

Alone in the Word You clearly speak
Alone in the promises to come and seek
Alone in the beauty that will not cease
Alone in the faithfulness found at Your Feet…

Show me, Lord, my life's end and the number of my days;
let me know how fleeting my life is.
Psalm 39:4

February 23
Take courage! It is I. Don't be afraid.
Mark 6:50

Seeing the Unseen
Not a ghost not a dream
Walking on the water in the storm
Teaching every moment beyond the norm

He knew their immediate need
Went beyond the storm to recede
That Peace in or out of the boat
Would keep their courage inwardly afloat

Power to change or bring calm
Ending the storm or giving a Psalm
Entrusted lessons given not earned
Wisdom from His Heart given to learn

Days continue as designed
Seasons arrive as assigned
Morning Mercies to remind
Sufficient Grace is there to find

I waited patiently for the Lord; He turned to me and heard my cry.
He lifted me out of the slimy pit, out of the mud and mire;
He set my feet on a Rock and gave me a firm place to stand.
Psalm 40:1-2

February 24
What do You want my heart to hear
There's more ahead do not fear
What do You want my heart to know
There's more treasure than any could hold

What do You want my heart to believe
There's more abundance than even greed
What do You want my heart to pray
There's more interwoven than words can say

What do You want my heart to comprehend
There's more beauty that never ends
What do You want my heart to sing
There's more found than lost in thanksgiving

Give thanks to the Lord, for He is good;
His Love endures forever.
Psalm 118:1, 29

Here's my heart, O take and seal it;
Seal it for Thy courts above.
-Come Thou Fount by Robert Robinson, 1758

February 25
In everything give thanks…
1 Thessalonians 5:18

In everything Lord really everything
Yes My child with thanksgiving
Thankful even for things I do not understand
Yes My child there I will always hold your hand

Thankful even for things I did not choose
Yes My child thankfulness inwardly restores and renews
Thankful even for things that hurt
Yes My child even then you will see My work

Thankfulness even when I'm so confused
Yes My child no prayer is ever refused
Thankfulness even when my heart is broken
Yes My child I mend with My Word already spoken

Thank You Father God for the way You sustain
Thank You for authentically bringing about change
Thank You for more than I can even or ever grasp
Yes, My child, trust My ways in everything you ask…

February 26
May you feel His love unending
In the song His Heart is sending
To comfort your heart and hold your hand
Through each moment so hard to understand

May you feel His love surround
In the song His Heart resounds
Being closer than each breath
In each moment your heart is met

By day the Lord directs His love,
at night His song is with me a prayer
to the God of my life.
Psalm 42:8

Hear our prayer, O Lord
Incline Thine ear to us
And grant us Thy peace
Amen
-Anonymous

February 27
Thank You for winter butterflies
That miraculously flutter so alive
Announcing new life that will surely come
When the dead of winter is ordained as done

Thank You for reminders meant to see
Your faithfulness so tenderly
Neath the shadow of Your wing
Sheltered there in unending Spring

On my bed I remember You;
I think of You through the watches of the night.
Because You are my Help, I sing in the shadow of Your wings.
I cling to You; Your right hand upholds me.
Psalm 63:6-8

February 28
You know the timing and the when
You know the details of now until then
You know the needs that will fall into place
You know the moments each filled with Grace

Let us trust as we do not know
The moments ahead that You will direct and show
Let us remember You are in charge of time
And won't forget one detail's design

Trusting You for the plans of this week
Already made but perhaps not for my feet
Trusting to go wherever You lead
And know that is where You will meet each need

*The Lord replied,
"My Presence will go with you,
and I will give you rest."
Exodus 33:24*

(February 29)
His Heart wreath
Hung for keeps
In remembrance of
His daily love

His autumn leaves
Fell with ease
Forming a heart
His work of art

His guided wind
Directed to send
Appointed Grace
Gathered and placed

His Heart motion
Is settled devotion
Letting eyes see
His Heart endlessly

I have loved you with an everlasting love;
I have drawn you with unfailing kindness.
Jeremiah 31:3

MARCH

March 1
A lamp unto my feet
Where my life is found complete
Guided through the darkest night
Never without Your inextinguishable Light

A lamp You alone provide
To be my Everlasting Guide
Mercy that tends and lights the way
To mend so gently throughout each day

A lamp of Lovely set in place
To redirect and guide my pace
Toward the coming of Your embrace
With undimmed Light to complete the race

Your Word is a lamp for my feet,
a light on my path.
Psalm 119:105

March 2

...being fully persuaded
that God had the power to do what He had promised.
Romans 4:21

That God...has and does
That God...Is and Was
That God...shall and will
That God...promises fulfill

That God...my heart song
That God...my Rest each dawn
That God...my Hope and Stay
That God...my Strength each day

Dawn is the work of His endless song
Given a glimpse of glory that belongs
Higher and deeper than hearts can know
From the One Who loves each so

Noon is the brightest that can be found
Noisily busily bodies abound
Brightness almost always ignored
By the Hand that ever supplies more

Dusk the quieted time that's given
Unto the slowness of the driven
Winding down to a rhythm of blessed
From the Giver of Sabbath Rest

Night the time the stars are seen
Perhaps as vivid as sweet dreams
The Faithful Witness set within His lullaby
To sing over hearts until dawn draws nigh…

*Once for all, I have sworn by My holiness and I will not
lie to David that his line will continue forever and his throne
endure before Me like the sun; it will be established forever
like the moon, the faithful witness in the sky.
Psalm 89:35-37*

March 3
The lone bluebonnet
Chosen like a sonnet

To enjoy with eyes
As feet move close by

Remembrance of springs' embrace
In the bouquets of seeded pace

Reassurance that deep within
Perennial beauty has come again

Bursting forth above the ground
Celebrating the seasonal sound

That once again a seed that died
Has reproduced all Texas-sized

Chosen to conclude this sonnet
Is this beautiful lone bluebonnet

Very truly I tell you,
unless a kernel of wheat falls to the ground and dies,
it remains only a single seed.
But if it dies,
it produces many seeds.
John 12:24

March 4
His Heart on that tree
Died willingly
His Heart on that tree
Surrendered intentionally

His Heart on that tree
Set mine free
His Heart on that tree
Gave graciously

His Heart on that tree
Outstretched for me
His Heart on that tree
Forgives perfectly

His Heart on that tree
Still speaks mercifully
His Heart on that tree
Says, "Come unto Me!"

Come unto Me…
and I will give you rest.
Matthew 11:28

March 5
Assign to each man the specific things he is to carry.
Numbers 4:23

Kohathites appointed to carry but not touch
They knew the privilege of holding such
The reverence of the holy articles within the tent
Was how their strength and life was spent

Jesus appointed to carry and touch
The holiness of Heaven to reach each of us
The wholeness of uncontainable Grace
Is how His intended can experience His Face

For this God is our God for ever and ever;
He will be our Guide even to the end.
Psalm 48:14

Christ the power of God and the wisdom of God.
1 Corinthians 1:24

March 6
*Therefore He is able to save completely
those who come to God through Him,
because He always lives to intercede for them.
Hebrews 7:25*

"Completely" that settled in my heart as I read
His ability NEVER mine instead
"Completely" a word that leaves no missing part
Over any circumstance of my heart

"Completely" the thought is not only Peace
But a resting reminder of His provisional Strength
"Completely" the inclusiveness of being made whole
Meeting the most desperate need within my soul

March 7

Because You are my Help,
I sing in the shadow of Your wings.
My soul clings to You;
Your right Hand upholds me.
Psalm 63:7-8

They introduced me to You
Teaching that You will carry me through
They introduced me to sing unto
The Heart of and for You

They introduced footsteps to follow and bring
The song of thanksgiving as my offering
They introduced the shadow of Your Wing
Where my heart can still hear their voices sing

(My beloved parents introduced my heart to the Giver of music)

March 8

So He sent two of His disciples telling them, "Go into the city, and a man carrying a jar of water will meet you. Follow him. Say to the owner of the house he enters, 'The Teacher asks: Where is My guest room, where I may eat the Passover with My disciples?' He will show you a large room upstairs, furnished and ready. Make preparations for us there.
Mark 14:13-15

My guest room already prepared
Furnished completely in the upstairs
For My disciples and I to dine
One last final Passover time

My guest room I guided a heart to prepare
So I alone could meet with My beloved twelve there
Wanting to spend this last Amen
Before I became the Lamb for each of them

My guest room I wanted each to be prepared to know
My Heart loved each no matter where they were about to go
That I came specifically to be recorded and show
Forgiveness in a way that all sins are atoned…

Fast forward later many years…
My unending message being made clear…
Through the decades reaching to…
The generation now holding you…

My heavenly guest room is prepared for your very heart
Awaiting for the wedding feast to begin and start
Where you will behold Grace forever with perfected eyes
My gift to you the Lamb once slain unendingly Alive…

(Until then I pray…)
Create in me a clean heart, O God;
and renew a right spirit within me.
Psalm 51:10 AKJV

March 9
(Now Moses was a very humble man, more humble than anyone else on the face of the earth.)
Number 12:3

How a man can completely change
From murderer to be called by name
How a man can come to the end of himself
To be useful in saving someone else

How a man can walk away
To be taught to lead God's way
How a man can find true identity
Listening to God's voice unendingly

How a man can be guided through
Following wholly the Lord that's true
How a man will not stay the same
Following Unseen footsteps that imprint change

With humility comes wisdom.
Proverbs 11:2b

March 10

*Speak to the Israelites and say to them:
"After you enter the land I am giving you as a home then the
person who brings an offering shall present to the Lord..."
Numbers 15:2, 4*

God in His gracious plan
Spoke the future to the hearts of man
Speaking the words "after" and "then"
To the generation that would not listen to Him

As the forty year wilderness moments began
God in His goodness spoke of its end
What could be expected as true
In spite of the unbelief they had fallen into

Yet God would not cut off His Covenantal plan
That He had spoken about the promise land
Nor the lineage threaded through men
Imperfect hearts chosen for "after" until "then"

God's "then"...
*He has helped His servant Israel,
remembering to be merciful to Abraham
and his descendants forever,
just as He promised our ancestors.
Luke 1:54-55*

God's "then"…
So Joseph also went up from the town of Nazareth in Galilee to Judea, to Bethlehem the town of David, because he belonged to the house and line of David. He went there to register with Mary, who was pledged to be married to him and was expecting a child. While they were there, the time came for the baby to be born, and she gave birth to her firstborn, a son. She wrapped him in cloths and placed him in a manger, because there was no guest room available for them.
Luke 2:4-7

God's way is perfect.
The Lord's promise always proves to be true.
He protects those who trust in Him.
Psalm 18:30 ERV

He took him outside and said, "Look up at the sky and count the stars if indeed you can count them." Then He said to him, "So shall your offspring be."
Genesis 15:5

March 11

Thank You for what once was that is no more
Moments that are reminders of Grace outpoured
Giving me strength when I had none
Holding my heart when I was undone

Thank You for letting me look back to see
Your faithfulness given directly to me
In ways that grew my life to depend
On knowing Your love simply has no end

Thank You for taking the time to show
Intentional love You wanted me to know
For carrying me through my hardest days
And Shepherding my heart in countless ways

*Surely God is my help,
the Lord is the One Who sustains me.
Psalm 54:4*

March 12
Thus the heavens and the earth were
completed in all their vast array.
Genesis 2:1

Completed in all their vast array
Perfection created in just six days
But chapter three is the beginning of the end
When God made man with the option of obedience or sin

Love allowed the fall of man
Love had planned nail-scarred Hands
Love desires full surrender
Loves does not demand but is tender

Love cherished what He made
Love perished through the life He gave
Love arose on that third day
Love is from the Heart of Yahweh

Love shines through all the brokenness
Love shows hearts repeated faithfulness
Love redeems the lost forever found
Love completes in a vastness that astounds

March 13

*But the Lord said to Moses and Aaron,
"Because you did not trust in Me as holy in
the sight of the Israelites, you will not bring
this community into the land I give them."
Numbers 20:12*

How vital to follow God's commands
Ask Moses who could not enter the promised land
How vital to obey not optional
Ask Joshua and Caleb who believed the impossible

How vital to listen and obey
Ask Adam and Eve who were led astray
How vital to be honest in what is provided
Ask Ananias and Sapphira what they decided

How vital to immediately believe
Ask Zechariah who for months could not speak
How vital to grow in trust unhindered
Ask David who wrote his Psalm of surrender

How vital to draw the line in the sand
Ask the woman caught in adultery without the man
How vital the footprints to follow each day
Ask seeking then find His unending Way

Many have undertaken to draw up an account of the things that have been fulfilled among us, just as they were handed down to us by those who from the first were eyewitnesses and servants of the Word. With this in mind, since I myself have carefully investigated everything from the beginning, I too decided to write an orderly account for you, most excellent Theophilius, so that you may know the certainty of the things you have been taught.
Luke 1:1-4

These things I have spoken to you,
that in Me you may have peace.
John 16:33 NKJV

March 14

I will take refuge in the shadow of Your wings.
Psalm 57:1

In true surrender come along
Following the Shepherd's Song
Trusting in the heights and depths
Inwardly outwardly therein kept

In true surrender be mobilized
Following the Shepherd with fixed eyes
Every valley's staff-led steps
Safely through your east from west

For as high as the heavens are above the earth,
so great is His love for those who fear Him;
as far as the east is from the west,
so far has He removed our transgressions from us.
Psalm 103:11-12

March 15

Then the Lord opened the donkey's mouth, and it said to Balaam, "What have I done to you to make you beat me these three times?"
Balaam answered the donkey, "You have made a fool of me! If only I had a sword in my hand, I would kill you right now."
The donkey said to Balaam, "Am I not your own donkey, which you have always ridden, to this day? Have I been in the habit of doing this to you?"
"No," he said. Then the Lord opened Balaam's eyes, and he saw the angel of the Lord standing in the road with his sword drawn. So he bowed low and fell facedown.
Numbers 22:28-31

Numbers houses an amazing storyline
With blinded eyes closed sometimes like mine
Not seeing right in front of me
What a donkey could…unswervingly

God in His mercy openly let the donkey talk
Explaining the wisdom of his three stops
Balaam more concerned with his pain than the trip
How many times have I too let conviction slip

Thank You for the donkey lesson today
To let me see and hear You speak in this way
Open my heart before my mouth
Turning my compass True North not south

Keep my needy feet redirected
In Your chosen pace prepared and protected
To be Your willing vessel obediently
Without need of a donkey talking to me

Then I turned the page
And saw the opposite engaged
A man unable to speak for nine months
Until God's promise became his wife's baby bump

Cannot imagine the quietness
That took place in God's moment of this
Teaching His unending ways
In words He gave to be relayed

No matter how many times Zechariah tried
There was no sound from him supplied
Until he declared the baby is named John
Then immediately his voice was heard clear and strong

Openly praising the One
Who had given them their son
All who lived at that time
Heard firsthand what we still find

God works in ways mysteriously
Touching hearts continuously
God's timing gave and took away
The voice boxes to be heard in His miraculous way

...because of the tender mercy of our God, by which the rising sun will come to us from heaven to shine on those living in darkness and in the shadow of death, to guide our feet into the path of peace.
Luke 1:78-79

March 16
When my heart is crushed
It's Yours that's never rushed
When my spirit cries
It's Yours that replies

When my words are gone
It's Yours that strengthen each dawn
When my way is so hindered
It is Yours that helps my steps remember

But I will sing of Your Strength, in the morning I will sing of Your love; for You are my Fortress, my Refuge in times of trouble.
Psalm 59:16

Just A Closer Walk With Thee
-Anonymous, 1940

Show me Your ways, Lord, teach me Your paths.
Guide me in Your truth and teach me, for You are
God my Savior, and my hope is in You all day long.
Psalm 25:4-5

March 17
The line of Korah, however, did not die out.
Numbers 26:11

Mercy there was great and grace was free
Pardon there was multiplied to me
There my burdened soul found liberty, At Calvary
-William R. Newell, 1895

Because William's father sought his son to change
My heart knows this familiar refrain
Because once a prodigal that came to know
My heart too knows this message that flows

Because of the contrast of being saved
My heart too knows the power over the grave
Because of the mercy and pardon extended to William
My heart was taught this mercy anthem

Because Your Mercy was written and read
My heart knows pardon in my stead
Because You let Your Son willingly die
My heart has His Blood eternally applied

March 18
Trust Me this day
Trust as you go your way
Trust knowing My Heart is there
Trust Me as you go everywhere

Trust Me in every concern
Trust Me in what's yet to be learned
Trust Me in what you don't understand
Trust that I am holding your hand

Trust that I fully know
Trust that I am with you as you go
Trust that today is perfectly timed
Trust that you are fully Mine

Do not fear,
for I have redeemed you;
I have summoned you by name;
you are Mine.
Isaiah 43:1

March 19
Indeed You always are
Giving always from near not far
Changing always night from day
Moving always in hearts of clay

Goodness always You provide
Helping always hearts inside
Mercy always found from You
Forgiveness always Your gift that renews

I keep my eyes always on the Lord.
With Him at my right hand, I will not be shaken.
Psalm 16:8

March 20

You, God, are my God, earnestly I seek You;
I thirst for You, my whole being longs for You,
in a dry and parched land where there is no
water. On my bed I remember You; I think
of You through the watches of the night.
Because You are my help; I sing in the shadow
of Your wings. My soul clings to You;
Your right hand upholds me.
Psalm 63:1, 6-8

You are there to be sought
Hearing my every silent thought
You are there throughout each day
Holding my hand each step of the way

You are my Living Water
Speaking to Your fully known daughter
You are my Watcher through darkness of night
Delivering me through Your inextinguishable Light

You are the Song You give me to sing
Reminding my heart of the healing You bring
You are the Hand upholding mine
Leading in steps that strengthen on time

March 21
And having disarmed the powers and authorities,
He made a public spectacle of them,
triumphing over them by the Cross.
Colossians 2:15

Jesus disarmed with His outstretched arms
Any form of punishment or harm
Nothing can separate or stand in the way
Of Jesus Christ that conquered to save

Thank You for Your Word that says so
The Truth revealed for ALL to know
The Mercy nailed to willingly show
The Grace given for Life bestowed

Thank You for the faith to believe
Every Word that You speak
Giving Life through Your death
Spoken through Your final breath

Thank You that You rose again
Giving Hope destroying sin
Paying the debt no one else could
Taking our place for where debtors stood

March 22
Those who know Your Name trust in You, for You,
Lord, have never forsaken those who seek You.
Psalm 9:10

She knows Your Name and You know hers
She trusts in You and Hope is secure
She knows You will never leave nor forsake
She trusts in the promise of Your resting shade

She knows and seeks Your Holy Face
She trusts in Your unending Grace
She knows each breath You alone ordain
She trusts Your Heart with hers to sustain

She knows not the path of this unknown
She trusts therein Your leading alone
She knows there's no place You will not be
She trusts Your Heart unendingly

Blessed are those who keep His statutes
and seek Him with all their heart
Psalm 119:2

My soul is weary with sorrow;
strengthen me according to Your Word.
Psalm 119:28

My comfort in my suffering is this:
Your promise preserves my life.
Psalm 119:50

I have sought Your Face with all my heart,
be gracious to me according to Your promise.
Psalm 119:58

May Your unfailing love be my comfort, according to Your
promise to Your servant.
Psalm 119:76

March 23

*Then He arose and rebuked the wind,
and said to the sea, "Peace, be still!"
And the wind ceased and there was a great calm.
Mark 4:39 NKJV*

Thank You for the gift to speak
And for Your Word spoken as peace
Here am I so in need
Hold my hand take the lead

Thank You for the gift to know
Unfailing Love You came to show
Here am I so in need
Give me faith to still believe

Thank You for the gift to hear
Your Word intentional close and near
Here am I so in need
Teach my heart to listen then breathe

Breath of Heaven
-Chris Eaton, 1991

*He will quiet you with His Love…
Zephaniah 3:17*

March 24
The morning rest in the rain
The quieted steps therein changed
The nourishment for the dry ground
The graciousness of the mercy sound

The thunder rumbling softly there
The raindrops falling like answered prayer
The blessing coming graciously toward
The Gardener's tending His grace outpoured

Be glad, people of Zion, rejoice in the Lord your God,
for He has given you the autumn rains because He is faithful.
He sends you abundant showers, both autumn and spring rains, as
before.
Joel 2:23

March 25
You are not only Creator but the Replenisher
You do not have to but You desire to
You are not only the Giver but the Sustainer
You do not answer to any but are the Answer

You are not only Salvation but also the Sacrifice
You chose to die so others could choose to live
You are not only Holy but came to leave sinless footprints
You chose humility so hearts could receive You…

And they cried in a loud voice: "Salvation belongs to our God, who sits on the throne, and to the Lamb." "…saying: "Amen! Praise and glory and wisdom and thanks and honor and power and strength be to our God for ever and ever. Amen!
Revelation 7:10, 12

I will sing to the Lord all my life: I will sing praise to my God as long as I live.
May my meditation be pleasing to Him, as I rejoice in the Lord.
Psalm 104:33-34

March 26
One cannot fathom how Mighty yet near
Your Presence so close to bottle every tear
One cannot fathom how You could come
To be made flesh yet sinless like no one

One cannot fathom but only believe
Through faith You alone give to receive
One cannot fathom Grace so great
That a King would reverse what sin separates

One cannot fathom the depth of Mercy found
Only the graciousness that wholly surrounds
One cannot fathom such kindness drawing near
But can see this very Love written to hear…

*So then faith comes by hearing,
and hearing by the Word of God.
Romans 10:17*

*These things I have written to you who
believe in the Name of the Son of God,
that you may know that you have eternal
life, and that you may continue to believe
in the Name of the Son of God.
1 John 5:13 NKJV*

Then sings my soul…
-Carl Boberg, 1885

March 27

There's no part of our lives untouched
By our Savior Who loves each so much
There's never a true lack
Looking back over our past

There's a knowing that comes with age
That His goodness is present in every stage
There's a growing a surrendering within
Reflecting His Grace that always has been…

As your days, so shall your strength be.
Deuteronomy 33:25 NKJV

A wonderful Savior is Jesus my Lord
He taketh my burden away
He holdeth me up, and I shall not be moved
He giveth me strength as my day
-Fanny Crosby, 1890

March 28
Forgive my doctrine of unbelief
For believing You wouldn't be my Hope and Strength
Forgive my lessons I in anger taught
For believing that Your love had truly stopped

Forgive the doubt and fears I owned
For believing I was forsaken and all alone
Forgive the burdens I held onto
For believing You wouldn't carry me through

Thank You for Your doctrine of faith and belief
Thank You for meeting me in my grief
Thank You for forgiveness that day
Thank you for taking my burdens away

Thank You for the gift in time
That lassoed back my heart soul and mind
Thank You for waiting tirelessly
For my heart to find Rest only in Thee…

Never will I leave you; never will I forsake you.
Hebrews 13:5

March 29
You keep Your Song so very near
That my heart can continue to hear
The Truth You are and have made known
That You are forever Sovereign alone

You allow Your perfect Rest
To be the place of honestness
Where You invite authentically
Shalom that covers unendingly

You amaze and fill my heart
With words You speak and impart
That fill each empty longing space
Within the infiniteness of Your Grace

*You will keep in perfect peace him whose
mind is steadfast, because he trusts in You.
Isaiah 26:3*

Perennial Peace Perennial Strength
Perennial Embrace Perennial Grace

Perennially met Perennially kept
Perennially owned Perennially known

Perennial Rest Perennial blessed
Perennial Shalom Perennially shown

March 30
You never run out of words
To be lived to be heard
You never run out of Water that flows
From Heaven's Throne to accept and know

You never run out of Your pursuit
For the lost to know Your Truth
You never run out of precious time
For today's premiere pricelessly designed

Be my Rock of Refuge, to which I can always go.
Psalm 71:2

For You have been my Hope, O Sovereign Lord,
my confidence since my youth.
Psalm71:5

March 31
The quiet is where I long to stay
In this morning moment of the day
Resting within each word You speak
Ever available timelessness within reach

Thank You for Your gift of calm
That is a forever familiar song
Of Peace on earth You unendingly give
Imprinted on hearts to truly live

Peace I leave with you;
My Peace I give you.
John 14:27

When peace like a river attendeth my way,
When sorrows like sea billows roll;
Whatever my lot, Thou hast taught me to say,
"It is well, it is well with my soul."
-Horatio Gates Spafford, 1873

April

April 1

Thank You for the distance between
The desired outcome and its happening
That time allotted to wholly see
Your plan and purpose intentionally

Thank You for the distance between
That may not turn out as I had dreamed
But this I experientially have come to trustingly know
Your ways are perfect and unceasingly show…

The afterward of the distance between
The afterward Your long-awaited dream
The afterward of Your forever embrace
The afterward of visible and merciful Grace

Yet I am always with You,
You hold me by my right hand.
You guide me with Your counsel, and afterward
You will take me into glory. Whom have I in Heaven but You?
And earth has nothing I desire besides You.
My flesh and my heart may fail,
but God is the strength of my heart and my portion forever.
But as for me, it is good to be near God.
I have made the Sovereign Lord my refuge;
I will tell of all Your deeds.
Psalm 73:23-26, 28

Here I Am To Worship
-Tim Hughes, 1999

April 2

But God is my King from long ago; He brings salvation on the earth. **It was You** *who split open the sea by Your power; You broke the heads of the monster in the waters.* **It was You** *who crushed the heads of Leviathan and gave it as food to the creatures of the desert.* **It was You** *who opened up springs and streams; You dried up the ever-flowing rivers. The day is Yours, and Yours also the night; You established the sun and moon.* **It was You** *who set all the boundaries of the earth; You made both summer and winter.*
Psalm 74:12-17

It was You behind and making each scene
It was You providing the healing stream
It was You nurturing all that was made
It was You becoming the sheltering shade

It was You establishing the day from night
It was You guiding with inextinguishable light
It was You giving the first and last song
It was You longingly lovingly all along

April 3
The unexpected that comes our way
Is not unexpected to the One we pray
He knows what's coming when we do not
And the duration before it stops

The unexpected can mold and shape
In unexpected ways our growing faith
Teaching us to expectantly know
That He is working good within our soul

And we know that in all things God works
for the good of those who love Him,
who have been called according to His purpose.
Romans 8:28

April 4

I lift up my eyes to the mountains where does my help come from? My help comes from the Lord, the Maker of heaven and earth. He will not let your foot slip He who watches over you will not slumber; indeed, He who watches over Israel will neither slumber nor sleep. The Lord watches over you the Lord is your shade at your right hand; the sun will not harm you by day, nor the moon by night. The Lord will keep you from all harm He will watch over your life; the Lord will watch over your coming and going both now and forevermore.
Psalm 121:1-8

Psalm One hundred twenty-one began this day
The one that You have graciously made
To walk upon and be held within
From beginning without end

As I rise to be guided through
The graciousness that You choose
My heart is lifted high
As You alone give Your reply

Live this day that I gave
Lean into My sheltering shade
Watch and see My Hand holding you
Feel My Grace carrying you through

Then you…you shall rejoice in all the good things the Lord your God has given to you and your household.
Deuteronomy 26:11

Have Thine own way Lord,
Have Thine own way
Thou art the Potter I am the clay
Mold me and make me, after Thy Will
while I am waiting yielded and still..

Wounded and weary, help me I pray
Power all power, surely is Thine
Touch me and heal me, Savior Divine
Adelaide A. Pollard, 1907

Peace, Peace wonderful Peace
Coming down from the Father above
Sweep over my spirit forever I pray
In fathomless billows of love
W. D. Cornell, 1888

April 5

Is the wind Your breath and sigh
Given there for wings to fly
Is the music Your harmony
Given there for worshiping

Is the spring Your holy dance
Given there for new life's chance
Is the quiet Your instrument
Given there for contentment

Is the harbor Your appointed Rest
Given there for weariness
Is the journey Your rhythmic pace
Given there for unending Grace

Is the pasture Your setting apart
Given there for shepherded hearts
Is the timeline Your gracious way
Given there for finding You each day

Is the compassion Your mercy to find
Given there for when life doesn't rhyme
Is the storm Your way to speak
Given there for knowing Peace

In repentance and rest is your salvation,
in quietness and trust is your strength.
Isaiah 30:15

April 6

Behold! The Lamb of God who takes away the sin of the world!
John 1:29 NKJV

You agreed to be the Passover Lamb
You the Holy of Holies and Great I AM
You agreed to suffer and die
You the Sinless One for I

You agreed to Calvary
You the King of Royalty
You agreed to Salvation bring
You the Author of Sovereignty

It is the Lord's Passover.
Exodus 12:1 NKJV

April 7
Yet not as I will, but as You Will.
Matthew 26:39

Thank You that this day Your Will on earth was done
For us to be a part of Your Kingdom come
Thank You for letting go of Your Son
For us to be in Your Kingdom as one

Thank You for the Cross Jesus bore
For us to be forgiven in Your Kingdom forevermore
Thank You for Your Good on the appointed Friday
For us to be restored in Your Kingdom always

Our Father in Heaven,
Hallowed be Your Name.
Your Kingdom come, Your Will be done
on earth as it is in Heaven.
Matthew 6:9-10 NKJV

April 8
You made and are making all things new
In and through the sacrifice of You
In Your final words and final breath
You restored and renewed through death

This Was and Is a continual Gift to receive
Everlasting Life merciful Grace from Thee
This moment the reason that You came
To take and remove all sin all shame

Oh Hallelujah be the song
For every soul to sing along
The "peace on earth" the angels sang
Was and Is the culmination of eternal change

Then He who sat on the throne said,
"Behold, I make all things new."
And He said to me, "Write, for these words are true and faithful."
Revelation 21:5 NKJV

April 9
Beautiful Your sunrise to see
Purposeful in Your Majesty
All of Heaven and its Glory
Telling Your forever Story

Written down for hearts to know
Grace and faithfulness that overflows
From Your Heart of Mercy's reign
Bringing forth forever change

Higher than Your thoughts above
Deeper than Your depths of love
Hands outstretched on Calvary
Grace's pardon mercifully

No tomb could ever hold You still
From accomplishing the Father's Will
Out You walked to freely give
Salvation for hearts to truly live

The Lord looks over us where He rules in Heaven.
Gazing into every heart from His lofty dwelling place.
Psalm 33:15 TPT

April 10
Standing in the cove of Grace
Finding Rest in what's embraced
The hidden quiet getaway
Before the day's new tidal wave

Here but a moment on Your earth You made
Growing neath Your Sheltering Shade
Finding Rest in Grace You provide
On the journey with You beside

We the sheep You are shepherding near
In Your footprints though unseen here
Upholding hearts to breathe and yearn
Within Your goodness we cannot earn

Granted footsteps in the pitch of praise
Your joyful accompaniment there always
Given for empty hearts to be filled
With Your Peace insurmountably instilled

Timelessly weaving in that hidden cove
Grace enough for each to know
Boundless fruitfulness You provide
In the pace of Your Rest inside

*Then we Your people, the sheep of Your pasture,
will praise You forever; from generation to generation
we will proclaim Your praise.
Psalm 79:13*

April 11

Walking in the dailyness
Of Your unending faithfulness
There the Grace to visually see
How Your shoulders carry me

Shepherd of my heart and soul
Safe within Your loving hold
Held forever like a song
Heard repeated as the dawn

Teaching my heart neath Your watch care
Nothing is missing with Your gift shared
Assurance of your Strength and Peace
Forms the cadence of my feet

There…in abandoned thankfulness
For new mercies of faithfulness
Perfectly placed forgiving Grace
In the grandeur of Your embrace

Whatever is true. Whatever is honorable
Whatever is right. Whatever is pure
Whatever is lovely…
Philippians 4:8

April 12

Thank You for what is meant to see
Every day intentionally
Thank You for what is meant to be heard
Every day found in Your Word

Thank You for what is meant to be owned
Every day rooted and sown
Thank You for what is meant to be known
Every day unendingly shown

Thank You for what is meant to be embraced
Every day such endless Grace
Thank You for what is meant to be found
Every day Hope that abounds

Everything I have is yours.
Luke 15:32

April 13

The moon moments there
Filling the night air
Until the greater light returns
Then its fading is discerned

The quiet moments there
Are most graciously shared
Through the changing of the guard
Outstretched globally over every yard

Timeless moments there
Outpouring Grace not spared
As Your Light illumines again
The candle-less glow that has no end

Thank You for the sun and moon
That cradles all both night and noon
Thank You for each ray that falls
Leaving us in holy awe

Thank you for Your Son that shines
Through every need graciously Divine
Thank You for such radiance
Every wonder beyond spontaneous…

Prompted to walk a different way
Chose to listen and obey
You had a wonder waiting there
That You wanted to graciously share

On My Way Home

Taking my feet toward the sun
What I saw left me undone
The forming of a radiant cross
The reason for my redirected walk

Where He leads I want to go
To see exactly what He will show
By His guiding to wholly land
Into His treasure moments planned

Thy Word is a lamp unto my feet and a Light…
Psalm 119:105

April 14

Every day so intentionally
You fill with Grace sufficiently
Every day so generously
You fill with Hope unendingly

Every day so faithfully
You fill with promise unmistakably
Every day so willingly
You fill with beauty actively

Every day so graciously
You fill with purpose unswervingly
Every day so tenaciously
You fill with kindness lovingly

Every day so intimately
You fill with devotion patiently
Every day so mercifully
You fill with You breathtakingly

Wrap your heart tightly around the Hope that lies within us, knowing that God always keeps His promises.
Hebrews 10:23 TPT

April 15

The ones that "threw" You away
You came to miraculously be emptied to save
The ones that fled and denied
You came to redeem and abide

The ones that wanted You to be dead
You came to multiply the fish and bread
The ones that refused to even hear
You came to ransom and draw near

The ones that blatantly falsely accused
You came to mercifully pardon and renew
The ones that emulated each sin found in us
You came to forgive…Thank You Jesus

*For there is one God and one mediator between
God and mankind, the man Christ Jesus, who gave
Himself as a ransom for all people.
1 Timothy 2:5-6*

April 16

Thank You for the words You spoke
Filling my heart with Your gift of Hope
Teaching to believe along the way
Your perfect timing appointed each day

Thank You for the words You speak
Filling my heart with joy complete
Teaching to believe all my days
Your perfecting timing and unending ways

Thank You for Your future words
Filling my heart clearly heard
Before the building was complete
Before the miracle of her feet

Thank You for each day You allow
Filling my heart with Hope right now
Teaching growing in the waiting days
Thankful for Your wisdom and perfect ways

As for God, His way is perfect:
The Lord's word is flawless.
Psalm 18:30

April 17

Fear not, for I am with you; be not dismayed,
for I am your God. I will strengthen you.
Yes, I will help you, I will uphold you with
My righteous right Hand.
Isaiah 41:10 NKJV

Speak these words into the depths
Into your heart where He is met
For His Heart is completely aware
Of your every heartache and every care

Believe His Help His Hand and Strength
Are greater than your ability to think
Look to the Heart that is near always
To Help you through what brings dismay

Fear not, for I am with you; be not dismayed,
for I am your God. I will strengthen you.
Yes, I will help you, I will uphold you with
My righteous right Hand.
Isaiah 41:10 NKJV

April 18

Give us hearts that see Yours sacredly
Give us hearts that hear Yours quietly
Give us hearts that approach Yours reverently
Give us hearts that follow Yours wholeheartedly

Give us hearts that cherish Yours unendingly
Give us hearts that obey Yours willingly
Give us hearts that seek Yours repeatedly
Give us hearts that trust Yours restfully

Give us hearts that find Yours assuredly
Give us hearts that praise Yours exceedingly
Give us hearts that acknowledge Yours longingly
Give us hearts that remember Yours unforgettably

Praise the Lord, O my soul and forget not…
Psalm 103:2

April 19
Come and sit for just awhile
Find needed Rest My dear child
Allow My Peace so quietly
To be heard in the depths of thee

Be still and know
My Grace overflows
Be still and rest
In My tenderness

Come and sit for just awhile
Find needed Strength My dear child
Through every breath that I allow
Remember My Presence is with you now

*...and lo, I am with you always
[remaining with you perpetually regardless
of circumstance, and on every occasion],
even to the end of the age.
Matthew 28:20*

There is a place of quiet rest
Near to the Heart of God...
-Cleland McAfee, 1903

April 20
Life lessons from a wordless bunny
You might think it "sounds" unusual or funny
But this creature has shown my heart this week
Many things without the ability to speak

You see a storm came today
And that bunny did not run away
She stayed in her exact chosen place
Protected from the rain even touching her face

The direction of the rain
Was like a liquid A-frame
Because she was beside the brick wall
The pouring rain didn't touch her at all

Then I began to observe deeper details
Than just a bunny with a white cottontail
In the choice that she decided
Made me see what Emmanuel provided

On My Way Home

The One that gives me a safe place to be
That protects within the storms decidedly
That is unending provision and Daily Bread
That is my Sustenance from toe to head

I know it's not about a bunny but she was used today
To teach my heart gratefulness for His loving ways
Provision of the Spirit never without
This is what "God with us" is all about

*And I will ask the Father, and He will give you another advocate
to help you and be with you forever the Spirit of Truth.
The world cannot accept Him,
because it neither sees Him nor knows Him.
But you know Him, for He lives with you and will be with you.
John 14:16-17*

April 21
Thank You for Your upwardness
That You placed in each of us
Eternally longing for You alone
To house our hearts before we are Home

Thank You for Your upwardness
Outstretched for every part of us
To unendingly satisfy and fill
With Peace that You alone instill

Thank You for Your upwardness
Reaching the deepest part of us
To live alive rejoicing each day
That You provided the Heart of Yahweh

He has made everything beautiful in its time.
He has also set eternity in the human heart; yet no one
can fathom what God has done from beginning to end.
Ecclesiastes 3:11

April 22

What do You awaken my eyes to see
New morning mercies of Your majesty
What do You awaken my ears to hear
New strength within that You are near

Where do You awaken my feet to go
In the footprints that You will show
Where do You awaken my heart to be
Held by You faithfully

When You awaken me You will sing
Rejoicing over me quietly as King
When You awaken me You will lead
Into Your Word for every need

You are Whom I awaken to hear
Made in Your image yet You draw near
You are Whom I awaken to meet
Strengthened by Your nail-driven Feet

When I awake, I am still with You.
Psalm 138:18

April 23

*He who dwells in the shelter of the Most High
will rest in the shadow of the Almighty. I will
say of the Lord, "He is my refuge and my fortress,
my God in Whom I trust."
Psalm 91:1-2*

Resting in the shadow of Your wing
Bringing my praise and thanksgiving
For the Rest that You alone give
Strengthening my heart to wholly live

Resting in the shelter of You Most High
Authentically hearing and knowing each cry
There's no other place given to safely dwell
Than in the foreverness of Emmanuel

April 24

What seems unfinished in my mind
Through Your sovereignty is perfectly timed
What whispered words I long to hear
Are authored by Your Heart so near

What mercy most needed for my stay
Your Life already has conveyed
What questions that linger deep inside
You answer with Peace that You provide

What seems uncertain is met in provisional care
You carrying each burden willingly shared
What comes unending as each new day
YOU faithfully leading in kindness always

For long ago the Lord had said to Israel: "I have loved you, O My people, with an everlasting love; with loving-kindness I have drawn you to Me."
Jeremiah 31:3 TLB

April 25
A ballerina learns that her spin
Has a focal point before she begins
The unrehearsed ballerina must learn the same
Or spinning will be what remains

A ballerina is filled with discipline
That exercises repeatedly without end
The unrehearsed ballerina finds the same
Ignored steps brings no dance of change

Thank You for letting me see today
My need for You in my spinning ways
Thank for being the steadfast place
For my eyes to focus on unending Grace

But You remain the same and Your years never end.
Psalm 102:27

April 26
Teach my heart to follow toward
In the direction of only Yours
Teach my feet to walk by faith
In the direction given to take

Teach my heart to willingly go
In the direction that You show
Teach my feet to align
In the direction where You refine

Teach my heart obedience's rhythm
In the direction You have graciously given
Teach my feet to continue on
In the direction You call upon

Teach my heart resting Peace
In the direction You grace with Strength
Teach my feet to follow toward
In the direction of only Yours

Teach me Your way, O Lord, I will walk and live in Your truth; direct my heart to fear Your Name [with awe-inspired reverence and submissive wonder].
Psalm 86:11 AMP

April 27
You lead in wonder every day
Purposed to see Your forgiving way
That frees a heart to graciously know
The Truth of Grace's endless flow

You show new wonders every dawn
Purposed for faith to lean upon
Encouraging hearts to be still and know
Unstoppable faithfulness of Mercy's flow

You teach through wonders to recognize
Perfect provision before watchful eyes
Instilling in hearts Your timing to know
Breathtaking moments that endlessly flow

Show me the wonders of Your great love,
You Who save by Your right Hand
those who take refuge in You from their foes.
Keep me as the apple of Your eye;
hide me in the shadow of Your wings…
Psalm 17:7-8

April 28
You bore every single part
Of our broken aching hearts
With faithfulness to carry on
Through Your Strength to lean upon

You bore thoroughly in every way
To hold each fast in every day
Whispering gently through every tear
For every heartache You are near

You bore each hurt so willingly
To be forever near unendingly
Taking on Yourself ALL grief of change
Leaving Your Spirit to walk inside our pain

You bore ALL to reveal through quieting Peace
Bringing calm as You graciously speak
Reminding hearts You understand
Through ALL that feels greater than

The Lord is close to the brokenhearted and
Saves those who are crushed in spirit.
Psalm 34:18

April 29

Know that the Lord is God.
It is He Who made us, and we are His,
we are His people, the sheep of His pasture.
Psalm 100:3

Know your Maker and King
Know your Creator of everything
Know your Savior that lived to die
Know your Salvation has come from on High

Know blessed assurance now and always
Know holiness and goodness from Yahweh
Know perfect redemption is His plan
Know forever Peace through nail-pierced Hands

For the Lord is good and His love endures forever;
His faithfulness continues through all generations.
Psalm 100:5

Blessed assurance Jesus is mine
Oh what a foretaste of glory divine
Heir of salvation purchase of God
Born of His Spirit washed in His Blood
-Fanny Crosby, 1873

April 30
Soundlessly the sun rises again
Shining forth faithfully as newness begins
Another day to rejoice within
Grateful that Your Light has no end

Thank You for the depths of Your healing each day
And for yesterday's layers that get peeled away
Allowing heart eyes in stillness to see
Unending Grace through Calvary's Tree

Thank You for tenderness at break of day
To be fully known then given away
From Your Heart of endless Power
Through Your kindness every hour

Thank You for Your songs in the night
Of mending rest You extend and ignite
Thank You for Your nearness that enfolds
Around the clock and never lets go

The Lord Himself goes before you and will be with you;
He will never leave you…
Deuteronomy 31:8

Jane Spears

May

May 1

He replied, "Why do you ask My Name?
It is beyond understanding."
Judges 13:18

Not only is Your Name beyond understanding
But also the blueprint of Grace in Your planning
The consummation of glory and grace
Was Galilean parents that first saw Your face

Thirty years You walked in anonymity
Until You began Your Gospel ministry
Then You asked hearts Yours to follow
So theirs would no longer live hollow

Your Name is still beyond understanding
But You reconciled all that Heaven was planning
The consummation of the human race
Was the empty tomb filled with redemptive Grace

For everyone has sinned;
we all fall short of God's glorious standard.
Yet God, in His grace, freely makes us right in His sight.
He did this through Christ Jesus when He freed us from the
penalty for our sins.
Romans 3:23-24 NLT

May 2
*Because he was very thirsty, he cried out to the Lord,
"You have given your servant this great victory.
Must I now die of thirst and fall into the hands of the
uncircumcised?"
Then God opened up the hollow place in Lehi, and water came out
of it.
When Samson drank, his strength returned and he revived.
Judges 15:18-19*

Teachable moments for each inherited breath
Is just as crucial as every step
That every movement and the how
Is through sufficient strength You alone allow

You are purposeful in what stretches here
Teaching through lingering Your Heart is near
In breathless moments so pain-filled
Your footprints lead and peace instill

You alone revive and restore
Renewing breath as never before
You alone lead through the valleys low
For breath to embrace the pace of slow

*Thanks be to God for His indescribable gift!
2 Corinthians 9:15*

May 3
Morning quiet wholly astounds
In Your faithfulness unendingly found
Placed exact for hearts and eyes
To know the Grace that Yours supplies

Appointed Heart to rescue and redeem
Through the intentional rugged crossbeams
Hanging upon the ever renowned tree
Purposed for objects of mercy to walk free

Morning quiet Your wholeness reminds
Come again to seek then find
My Heart in the center the middle ground
Where I once stood for My Grace to be found

*Two rebels were crucified with Him, one on
His right and one on His left.
Matthew 27:38*

May 4
The symbol of peace the olive branch
The touch of God's standard over each circumstance
Always giving and supplying visually
Gracious pure Love unconditionally

The olive grove that held The Branch
Willing to atone human circumstance
Continually gives supplying visually
Pure love and devotion unendingly

The olive branch we hold in our heart
Can replicate the forgiveness He alone imparts
By extending His kindness visually shown
Emulating His Grace that He makes known

To Him who loves us and has freed us from our sins by His Blood, and made us to be a kingdom and priests to serve His God and Father to Him be glory and power for ever and ever! Amen.
Revelation 1:5-6

Greater love has no one than this:
to lay down one's life for one's friends.
John 15:13

May 5
Shall there be a morning view
Shall there be a song that soothes
Shall there be a wingless wind
Shall there be a knee that bends

Shall there be a moment stilled
Shall there be a longing fulfilled
Shall there be a cry that is heard
Shall there be a comforting word

Shall there be a resting repose
Shall there be a solace composed
Shall there be a reaping sown
Shall there be a Fountain known

*We know that when Christ appears,
we shall be like Him,
for we shall see Him as He is.
1 John 3:2*

*For with You is the fountain of life;
in Your light we see light.
Psalm 36:9 NKJV*

May 6

*You know every step I will take before my journey even begins,
You've gone into my future to prepare the way, and in kindness
You follow behind to spare me from the harm of my past.
Psalm 139:3-4 TPT*

*Go ahead, my daughter.
Ruth 2:2*

Go ahead My daughter and soon you will find
Rest in My lineage I have in mind
Through Your kindness known to Naomi
My Story continues for you to also know Me

In your willingness to intentionally cleave
Showed your trust of residency
Leading back to My birthplace
Reflecting beforehand My coming Grace

Thank you for your promise kept
To leave and cleave in every step
Trusting in My ability to nourish
Leaning into steps purposed to flourish

Thank you for letting the whole town see
Devotion given so willingly
Walking away to embrace anew
My Kinsman-Redeemer awaiting you

*Do not fear, for I have redeemed you;
I have summoned you by name; you are Mine.
Isaiah 43:1*

May 7
Walk to listen breathe and glean
Basking in My new dawning scene
What I timed to perfectly be
Morning beauty among My trees

Perhaps you'll see the heart shape there
In My clouds like a winged prayer
That I formed to be recognized
As lovingly given and personalized

Everything I am will praise and bless the Lord!
O Lord, my God, Your greatness takes my breath away,
overwhelming me by Your majesty, beauty, and splendor.
Psalm 104:1 TPT

May 8
You alone give eyes to see
Dawning beauty from Your treasury
No cloud can remove or take away
The majesty You planned for this new day

Amazing Grace lighting each step
Unending forgiveness divinely met
Mercy given to find intricately
Hope once again all from Thee

Lost in such wonder yet held by Your Hand
Shepherding through as one of Your lambs
Allowing each scene as it brings change
To know assuredly Your Peace remains

Strengthening by such tenderness
That You provide for each of us
Until our eyes purely see
Your Heart alone as our Treasury

Praise the Lord.
Give thanks to the Lord, for He is good; His love endures forever.
Who can proclaim the mighty acts of the Lord or fully declare His praise?
Psalm 106:1-2

When we walk with the Lord
in the light of His Word
What a glory He sheds on our way...
-John Henry Sammis, 1887

May 9
Perfectly placed appointed time
Faithfulness experienced by design
The promise of the sunrise every day
To rest in Your goodness now and always

Perfect setting tenaciously kind
Leading by the Hand that graciously holds mine
Amazing to be held by the Giver of Light
That whispers bright Hope in the darkness of night

Never am I perfect only in blunders
Yet perfectly loved vast beyond numbers
Thank You for perfecting perennially
Through perfect Love given unconditionally

As for God, His way is perfect: The Lord's Word is flawless;
He shields all who take refuge in Him.
Psalm 18:30

Walking in sunlight, all of my journey,
over the mountains through the deep vale
Jesus has said, "I'll never forsake thee,"
promise divine that never can fail.
Heavenly sunlight, heavenly sunlight,
flooding my soul with glory divine;
Hallelujah, I am rejoicing,
singing His praises, Jesus is mine.
-Henry J. Zelley, 1899

May 10

But the people refused to listen to Samuel. "No!" they said.
"We want a king over us.
Then we will "be like" all the other nations, with a king to lead us
and to go out before us and fight our battles."
1 Samuel 8:19-20

Similar words heard spoken in Eden
Wanting to "be like" instead of following God's leading
There a subtle whispering of doubt
That each heart was being left out

Oh to have ears opened to hear
The Heartbeat leading through doubt and fears
He knows each need and provides
Without the need of fig leaves to hide

The Story unfolding though was preparing
All generations for His unending reigning
As the only One to "be like"
Through the Grace of Jesus Christ

Then Jesus declared, "I am the Bread of Life.
Whoever comes to Me will never go hungry,
and whoever believes in Me will never be thirsty."
John 6:35

Oh! To be like Thee, blessed Redeemer,
This is my constant longing and prayer;
Gladly I'll forfeit all of earth's treasures,
Jesus, Thy perfect likeness to wear.

Oh! To be like Thee, Oh! To be like Thee,
Blessed Redeemer, pure as Thou art;
Come in Thy sweetness, come in Thy fullness;
Stamp Thine own image deep on my heart.
-Thomas O. Chisholm, 1897

May 11

In all my agenda and tendencies
You let me see the importance of time with Thee
In all my plans that come to a halt
You let me experience faithfulness that does not stop

Thank You for gifts small yet great
That I forget to celebrate
Until they are on hold for a time
And I recognize how dependently I am designed

Give thanks to the Lord, His love endures forever.
He stilled the storm to a whisper; the waves of the
sea were hushed. They were glad when it grew calm,
and He guided them to their desired haven.
Let them give thanks to the Lord for His unfailing love
and His wonderful deeds for mankind.
Psalm 107:1, 29-31

Take my life and let it be, Consecrated Lord to Thee
Take my hands and let them move, At the impulse of Thy love…
Take my feet and let them be, Swift and beautiful for Thee
Take my voice and let me sing, always only for my King…
-Frances R. Havergal, 1874

May 12
My Presence will go with you, and I will give you rest.
Exodus 33:14

Let me follow on the path You provide
Not the ones that I have tried
Let me follow where You lead
In surrender of every need

Let my heart remember well
That Your Spirit forever indwells
Let my soul find rest again
In Your Word that heals within

Let me bloom like Your flowers
In the present by Your power
Let my steps be only toward
Only Yours forevermore

Let me choose Your gentle ways
Beginning to end in this new day
Let me hear Your unending refrain
Come find Rest in My Name

Come to Me, all you who are weary and burdened,
and I will give you rest.
Matthew 11:28

May 13

Is there a heart You want me to see
Yes all of Mine broken for thee
Is there a message You want to impart
Yes all of Mine engraved on your heart

Is there a pace You want me to know
Yes all of Mine both immediate or slow
Is there a promise You want me to hold
Yes all of Mine given and foretold

Is there a word You want me to speak
Yes all of Mine that give honor and peace
Is there a song You want me to sing
Yes all of Mine with thanksgiving

Is there a heartbeat You want me to hear
Yes all of Mine that are instilled and near
Is there a solace You want me to know
Yes all of Mine like a river that flows

As the deer pants for streams of water,
so my soul pants for You, my God.
By day the Lord directs His love, at night
His song is with me a prayer to the God of my life.
Psalm 42:1, 8

May 14
She took the time to pray
So I would know Jesus as mine someday
She took the time at Jesus feet
So I would know the gift of Peace

She took the time to truly know
So I would learn the Bible tells me so
She took the time to graciously live
So I would know the One Who forgives

She took the time to joyfully sing
So I would know Jesus as Lord and King
She took the time lovingly
So I would know Grace eternally

There is a time for everything…
Ecclesiastes 3:1

Jesus loves me this I know…
-Anna B. Warner, 1860

May 15

*David said to the Philistine,
"You come against me with sword and spear
and javelin, but I come against you in the Name of the Lord
Almighty, the God of the armies of Israel, whom you have defied.
All those gathered here will know that it is not by sword or spear
that the Lord saves; for the battle is the Lord's, and He will give
all of you into our hands."
1 Samuel 17:45-46*

The Philistine giant's description
Was no match for God's prescription
The details of height and measurement
Was no match for God's Testament

The taunt of the giant that was heard
Was no match for God's everlasting Word
The ground that would soon hold the giant's fall
Was no match for God's Might at all

The "giants" we face in our story
A personalized "rematch" to give God Glory
The height depth or length
Never can outmatch God's Power and Strength

*Greater is He that is in you, than he that is in the world.
1 John 4:4 KJV*

Great are the works of the Lord;
they are pondered by all who delight in them.
Glorious and majestic are His deeds,
and His righteousness endures forever.
He has caused His wonders to be remembered;
the Lord is gracious and compassionate.
Psalm 111:2-4

The fear of the Lord is the beginning of wisdom;
all who follow His precepts
have good understanding.
To Him belongs eternal praise.
Psalm 111:10

May 16
Walk aware
Of My Goodness already there
Breathe aware
Of My Mercy I share

Live aware
Of My Joy not spared
Listen aware
Of My attentive care

Walk there known
In My Goodness alone
Breathe sacred breath
In My restorative steps

Live joyously free
In My Sovereignty
Listen attentively well
In My identity dwell

On My Way Home

Walk as I lead
I know every need
Breathe as I sustain
I know every pain

Live as I lend
I know every bend
Listen as I speak
I know every grief

Walk humbly
Breathe reverently
Live justly
Listen fervently

He has shown you, O mortal, what is good.
And what does the Lord require of you?
To act justly and to love mercy and
to walk humbly with your God.
Micah 6:8

May 17
As my feet wind and go
Onto the path You already know
Remind my heart to once again praise
You alone for this new day

As my eyes behold and see
Sunshine and Hope You blend lovingly
Remind my heart You prepared this day
To begin and end in unhindered praise

As my mind begins to move
Into this moment prepared to choose
Remind my heart of purest devotion
Offered by Yours deeper than oceans

As my ears hear You speak
Imparting always unending Peace
Remind my heart You reserved this time
To praise Your Name as You refine

Let the Name of the Lord be praised, both now and forevermore.
From the rising of the sun to the place where it sets,
the Name of the Lord is to be praised.
The Lord is exalted over all the nations, His glory above the heavens.
Psalm 113:2-4

May 18
Treasure My timing given this day
Treasure My blessings sent your way
Treasure My moments each one anew
Treasure My gifts intended for you

Treasure My Presence with new eyes
Treasure My Sovereignty in each sunrise
Treasure My Goodness meant to be known
Treasure My Rest found in Me alone

Treasure My Intricacies that I appoint
Treasure My Word that I anoint
Treasure My Mercy given to find
Treasure My Footprints imprinted for thine

*"For My thoughts are not your thoughts,
neither are your ways My ways," declares the Lord.
"As the heavens are higher than the earth,
so are My ways higher than your ways and
My thoughts than your thoughts."
Isaiah 55:8-9*

Giver of immortal gladness,
fill us with the light of day...
-Henry Van Dyke, 1907

May 19

Such endless wonders of Your ways
Taught within at the break of day
Never space enough for doubt
That one single breath is overlooked or without

Can such faithfulness be described
That You graciously unendingly provide
Never a space where we are alone
Always Present forever known

Just as constant as the water's flow
Is Your Grace given to know
Your depth of solace and serenity
Given for always so lavishly

In Him we have redemption through His Blood,
the forgiveness of sins, in accordance with the riches of God's
grace that He lavished on us.
With all wisdom and understanding,
He made known to us the mystery of His Will according to His
good pleasure, which He purposed in Christ, to be put into effect
when the times reach their fulfillment —to bring unity
to all things in heaven and on earth under Christ.
Ephesians 1:7-10

May 20
Mary and Martha saw Your tears
The compassion from Your Heart very near
United in shared heartfelt grief
Demonstrating words without speech

Tears You allowed others to see
Feeling the depth of loss indeed
Not just back then but continually today
You are beside us now and always

What compassion in every grief
What tenderness that continually speaks
What an amazing moment of abiding Grace
For the testimony of tears running down Your Face…

Jesus wept.
John 11:35

For great is His love toward us,
and the faithfulness of the Lord endures forever.
Praise the Lord.
Psalm 117:2

May 21
I call to remembrance my song in the night;
I meditate within my heart.
Psalm 77:5 NKJV

My song in the night
Is Rest in Your sight
My song in Your Might
Is Rest in Your Light

My song that is heard
Is Rest in Your Word
My song that is Peace
Is Rest in Your Strength

The Lord is my strength and my song.
Psalm 118:14

May 22

You knew the Story before it was written
Your Heart toward dust was already smitten
Giving every drop of Your Blood
To show once and for all Unconditional Love

No penmanship could every write
Such Holiness of unending Light
That penetrates a heart and soul
Each time Your Story is retold

Your Words of Truth are written down
To quench the thirst of dusty dry ground
To learn Living Water washes away
What separated dust in Eden that day

And now the Spirit is the permanent seal
Of Jesus Christ and Grace revealed
Delivered and stamped with return to Sender
Saved by the Blood of our Kinsman-Redeemer

Do not fear, for I have redeemed you;
I have summoned you by name;
you are Mine.
Isaiah 43:1

Tell me the Story of Jesus,
write on my heart every word
-Fanny Crosby, 1880

May 23

*Jesus answered, "It is the one
to whom I will give this piece of bread
when I have dipped it in the dish."
Then dipping the piece of bread,
He gave it to Judas, the son of Simon Iscariot.
As soon as Judas took the bread,
Satan entered into him.
So Jesus told him, "What you are about to do, do quickly."
John 13:26-27*

Resolve of surrender began
When Jesus handed the bread to him
The permission granted to betray
Was given to Judas in that very way

Not only the resolve but power do I see
Jesus wasn't taken unwillingly
He knew the timing with intentionality
Of every detail leading up to Calvary

The Bread of Life gave His to give
His broken Body for all to live
Giving the bread into Judas' hand
Was the beginning of God's redeeming plan

On My Way Home

The awakening beauty graciously there
Gives pause to my steps to gaze and stare
At the unfolding of Your anointed plan
Visible grace from Your giving Hand

Appointed day of Your Kingdom come
Intentionality of Your Will be done
On earth as in the heavens that declare
Unconditional mercy provided to share

Then sings my soul in gratitude
Unable to comprehend Grace's latitude
Coming toward to lead to Your Throne
Filling each day with Your thoughts of Home

He will be the sure foundation for your times,
a rich store of salvation and wisdom and knowledge;
the fear of the Lord is the key to this treasure.
Isaiah 33:6

May 24
Teach me again to listen today
Teach me again to walk in Your ways
Teach me again there's always more
Teach me again of Your sovereignty Lord

Teach me again to trust anew
Teach me again to fix my eyes on You
Teach me again You alone sustain
Teach me again You know my name

Teach me again each goodness You send
Teach me again Your breath has no end
Teach me again newness to find
Teach me again what You have in mind

Teach me again You are patient each day
Teach me again nothing separates You from clay
Teach me again Your strengthening pace
Teach me again Your footprints of Grace

Show me Your ways, Lord, teach me Your paths.
Guide me in Your truth and teach me, for You are
God my Savior, and my Hope is in You all day long.
Psalm 25:4-5

Sing them over again to me, Wonderful words of life
Let me more of their beauty see, Wonderful words of life
Words of life and beauty, Teach me faith and duty
Beautiful words, wonderful words, Wonderful words of life
-P.P. Bliss, 1874

May 25

You move a body and a soul
In faithfulness You unendingly show
You move and mend each hurting heart
In faithfulness You alone impart

You move among continually
In faithfulness through Calvary
You move beside stilling the water
In faithfulness to every son and daughter

You move a mind to wholly receive
In faithfulness Your gift to believe
You move continually throughout each day
In faithfulness now and always

You move between each storyline
In faithfulness Your Grace to find
You move and soothe in perfect Peace
In faithfulness that will not cease

You move the weary wholly designed
In faithfulness Your reflection to find
You move within beside and before
In faithfulness forevermore

For the Word of the Lord is right and true;
He is faithful in all He does.
Psalm 33:4

May 26
Let me not race ahead but within Your pace
As my feet walk into this morning graced
Open my eyes to clearly see
Your loveliness more deeply

Drinking in the sight and sound
That You appointed to be found
The calm the quiet the sacred ground
Your Rest within for Your earthbound

Bringing each burden and each care
Gladly received by You tenderly there
Ever-present in every step
In the heights or in the depths

No place are we left on our own
Your promise is to never leave Your sheep alone
Your Heart goes with behind and before
Nothing hidden nothing ignored

Thank You for these moments shown
In this quiet given to be known
Such tenderness that continually comes
Within the identity as Your rest-filled one…

The Lord replied, "My Presence will go with you,
and I will give you rest."
Exodus 33:14

May 27
You are the Giver to every soul
Interceding that all would know
The Life You gave to wholly reach
Within the heart and soul of each

Individual love You graciously give
Individual pardon to wholly live
Individual Grace to fully know
Individual kindness that overflows

*When I consider Your heavens, the work of Your fingers,
the moon and the stars, which You have ordained,
what is man that You are mindful of him…
Psalm 8:3-4 NKJV*

*Therefore He is able also to save forever
(completely, perfectly, for eternity)
those who come to God through Him,
since He always lives to intercede and
intervene on their behalf [with God].
Hebrews 7:25 AMP*

May 28

Your Word, Lord, is eternal; it stands firm in the heavens.
Your faithfulness continues through all generations;
You established the earth, and it endures.
Your laws endure to this day for all things serve You.
If Your law had not been my delight, I would have perished in my affliction. I will never forget Your precepts, for by them You have preserved my life. To all perfection I see a limit, but Your commands are boundless.
Psalm 119:89-93, 96

Let each emotion find Rest in the Psalms
Words of comfort for every wrong
Timeless treasure found in each word
There to be read felt and heard

Spend time hearing and listening
Cling to the Peace His Word brings
Lay down the task of "in your own strength"
His arms already carried each burden to cease

He moved in such a miraculous way
That forgiveness is here every single day
The pain of sin in our here and now
He Grace-pierced through each thorn in His brow

May 29
All about God-given identity
Written down historically
So all would truly identically know
The Love of the Father for each as His goal

Made in His image from the beginning
To breathe His breath He gave so willing
To give each life His avenue of Grace
Before He created the human race

He knew each detail that would come
He knew His ultimate sacrifice for everyone
He knew there would be no substitute ram
He knew for the world He would be the Lamb

Help us remember the war that was won
Through the Blood of Jesus Your Son
You knew eternal freedom that would be gained
For every soul to know Your Name

Thank You for Your loving ways
In spite of the choices man has made
Thank You that You had the plan in place
For our brokenness to be redeemed by Your Grace

I am telling you what I have seen in the Father's presence…
John 8:38

O to be like Thee! O to be like Thee! Blessed Redeemer pure as
Thou art; Come in Thy sweetness, come in Thy fullness;
Stamp Thine own image deep on my heart.
-Thomas O. Chisholm, 1897

May 30
You still the waters to draw near
Deepening hearts to persevere
Not by might nor our power
But by Your Spirit strengthening each hour

You still the restless feet toward
Rest found only at Yours Lord
Teaching the prayer of surrender again
Thy Will be done is where to begin

You still the hunger there inside
By the provision You provide
Knowing the need before it becomes
Known in the depths of Your beloved ones

You still and quiet to wholly adhere
Within Your faithfulness intentionally near
Teaching solace as the pace
Deep within Your buoyancy of Grace

He leads me beside quiet waters,
He refreshes my soul…
Psalm 23:2a-3b

May 31
Let Your reflection repeatedly be
On display all glory unto Thee
Hidden under a bush "oh no!"
Let Your Light increasingly flow

From Your Heart that paved the way
For the wayward prone to stray
Finding Your footprints leading through
Until ours reflect only You

Highest heights or deepest depths
Both are places we are met
In Your Light to hear each time
Walk this way you are Mine

Let us find in the shadow of Thee
Perfect Peace continuously
Let our heart eyes intentionally see
Your Light unhindered unendingly

In Your light we see light.
Psalm 36:9b NKJV

This little light of mine, I'm gonna let it shine…
-Harry Dixon Loes, 1920

Jane Spears

JUNE

June 1

*For I am the Lord your God who takes hold of your right hand
and says to you, "Do not fear; I will help you."
Isaiah 41:13*

Truly You did and truly still do
Truly my Help is found only in You
Truly You knew and truly know
Truly the need found deep in my soul

Never a moment without Your care
Never a moment without You there
Never a moment to stand alone
Never a moment not met and known

Grateful tears testify now
In the looking back and seeing just how
Your faithfulness was there shaping my heart
In the knowledge that You would never depart

Thank You Lord for letting me see
Redeeming Love beyond degree
Taking my heartache and my pain
In exchange for Hope that remains

*Never will I leave you; never will I forsake you. So we say
with confidence, "The Lord is my Helper; I will not be afraid."
Hebrews 13:5-6*

June 2

This time is met and multiplied
Breadth of solitude You provide
This time is given to quietly abide
In each step You lead and guide

This time is to linger and to lean
As the morning unfolds like a dream
This time is to receive and to know
Graciousness that envelops and holds

This time is to be moved to be still
In boundless parameters that You fill
This time is to walk hearing within
Whispers of Hope once again

This time is to taste and truly see
Immeasurable kindness beautifully
This time is to keep pressing on
In Your tenderness timed each dawn

All this will be because the mercy of our God is very tender, and heaven's dawn is about to break upon us, to give light… and to guide us to the path of peace.
Luke 1:78-79 TLB

June 3
First sunflower alone blooming there
Awaiting what's already seeded to share
Ever tracking its Maker and King
Appointed timing its beauty be seen

May we like this sunflower be
Opening up in praise unto Thee
Heart eyes transfixed tracking time
In the cadence You designed

As we breathe Your solar gaze
In Your image each Heart-made
Implanted mercy each day's new rhyme
Grace reminders there to find

How unfathomable Your intentionality is
Tucked away wonders given like this
Faithful reminders through such intricacies
Given daily for heart eyes to see

I pray that the eyes of your heart may be enlightened...
Ephesians 1:18

June 4
Thank You that the journey is not aimless
That You infuse the ability to walk blameless
Cleansed and forgiven the Gift You impart
Purposed and planned to create a new heart

Though You knew the wayward feet
Would be lost and incomplete
Until the Resurrection of Your Son
When Mercy's Hope was victoriously won

There is not one without the need
For the vastness of His sacrificial deed
Covenant of Blood through surrendered Feet
Brought the Grace that forgiveness completes

As the deer pants for streams of water,
so my soul pants for You, my God.
My soul thirst for God, for the living God.
Psalm 42:1-2

Thank You Lord For Saving My Soul
-Seth and Bessie Sykes, 1940

June 5
No Light brighter or more fair
Than the kindness Your Heart shares
Like the rain that gently falls
Leaves my heart in wonder and awe

No place left untouched by the rain
Like Your Mercy You have proclaimed
Forgiveness a gift lovingly for all
Just like the thoroughness of the rainfall

Unpacked beauty meets my gaze
After the storm brings renewal and change
Reviving the dryness dependent on You
Unrivaled Hope as Grace-felt dew

I lift up my eyes to You,
to You whose throne is in Heaven.
...our eyes look to the Lord our God...
Psalm 123:1, 3

June 6

Job's response was to land in praise
Trusting and leaning into God's sovereign ways
He knew who had given all that he once had
And trusted God thoroughly through the good and the bad

He did not understand but still did not blame
The God of Heaven but worshiped His Name
Knowing God had a purpose and plan
Though he felt the heaviness of His Hand

What vertical trust and Hope we see
When all horizontal blessings vanish and flee
Out of sight and gone in a day
Still nothing could refute Job's surrender in praise

Job's life is the testimony of Have Thine Own Way
Surrendering himself in God's Hands as clay
Completely yielded completely still
Waiting and clinging to His purposed Will

An example of waiting when things are not intact
Lifting eyes not fists to unwanted facts
Acknowledging Who is truly in control
Complete surrender in Hands that never let go

*At this, Job got up and tore his robe and shaved his head.
Then he fell to the ground in worship and said:
"Naked I came from my mother's womb, and naked I will depart.
The Lord gave and the Lord has taken away;
may the Name of the Lord be praised."
In all this, Job did not sin by charging God with wrongdoing.
Job 1:20-22*

Have Thine own way, Lord
Have Thine own way
Thou art the Potter
I am the clay…
-Adelaide A. Pollard, 1906

June 7
In the archives of my heart
Forgetting not my appointed part
Recalling songs You gave in the night
Reviewing the words in the morning light

Placed within my heart to know
Echoing Grace within my soul
The song given not so long ago
Sweet reminder lovingly enfolds

Always Your plan to tenderly give
Echoing Grace extended to live
Teachable moments Your timing allows
Preparing hearts for more than just now

I remembered my songs in the night.
Psalm 77:6

Thank You that creation speaks Your Name
And that our hearts were made to do the same
We want to know You now
So we can praise You then
For You are more than we can comprehend
-To Know by Jane Spears 1998

June 8
There is Light continual to shine
There is Light continual to find
There is Light continual that leads
There is Light continual for each need

There is Light continual night or day
There is Light continual showing the way
There is Light continual by design
There is Light continual that refines

There is Light continual through the storm
There is Light continual that transforms
There is Light continual to recount
There is Light continual like a fount

There is Light continual through every hurt
There is Light continual through His work
There is Light continual sifting through the Hands of time
There is Light continual uplifting each heart to shine

When Jesus spoke again to the people,
He said, "I am the Light of the world.
Whoever follows Me will never walk in darkness,
but will have the Light of Life."
John 8:12

Here I Am To Worship by Tim Hughes, 1999

June 9
Such beauty such Peace
Awaiting steps of borrowed Strength
Walking beside faithful always
Through each need through each day

Such beauty such Grace
Awaiting moments of sacred space
For each trial therein found
Endless Hope that resounds

Such beauty such care
Awaiting breath in spoken prayer
For the answers that we seek
Met in gentleness before we speak

Such beauty such surrender
Awaiting memories that still and tender
Escorted along the inlet of calm
Where Hope begins new mercy's song

Praise be to God TODAY.
1 Kings 5:7

Morning by morning new mercies I see
All I have needed Thy Hand hath provided
Great is Thy Faithfulness, Lord unto me
-Thomas O. Chisholm, 1923

June 10
You bring quiet every dawn
You give the path to walk upon
You bring light to illumine the way
You give unendingly every day

Your bring sight to the blind
You give treasure then to find
You bring details in the clouds
You give joy to live out loud

You bring moments that fly away
You give wisdom to seek always
You bring more to drink within
You give hope that has no end

You bring solace through the storm
You give mercy daily reborn
You bring hearts perfect rest
You give strength in faltering steps

You bring a shell to inspect
You give time to reflect
You bring a purpose patterned there
You give slowness meant to share

You bring the turtle time to go
You give the terrain there bestowed
You bring hearts plain to see
You give joy unendingly

You make known to me the path of life;
You will fill me with joy in Your Presence
with eternal pleasures at Your right hand.
Psalm 16:11

June 11
Teach me to hear what You set in place
To listen to Your Song of Grace
Teach my heart to refocus well
Within the chambers You graciously dwell

Teach my feet to swiftly move
In the footsteps that You choose
Teach my eyes to see love IS blind
From Your forgiving Heart that forgives mine

Teach my soul Your faithfulness each day
Within Your Word for now and always
Teach my mind the rhythmic pace
Within the miracle of Gardening Grace

Trust in the Lord with ALL your heart…
Proverbs 3:5

On My Way Home

Come, every soul by sin oppressed,
there's mercy with the Lord;
And He will surely give you rest,
by trusting in His Word.
Only trust Him, only trust Him,
Only trust Him now…
-John Hart Stockton, 1874

Only trust Him indeed
Wherever you are let Him take the lead
He knows the moments your whole lifelong
Are shaping the lyrics for His song…

June 12
The hardest moments to walk through
The hardest moments we would not choose
The hardest moments of unknown length
The hardest moments saps known strength

Through hardest moments You fully know
Through hardest moments Your Heart enfolds
Through hardest moments You walk beside
Though hardest moments You unendingly abide

You, Lord, keep my lamp burning;
my God turns my darkness into light.
Psalm 18:28

Breath of Heaven by Chris Eaton, 1991

June 13
Moonless moment starless day
Cannot thwart unstoppable praise
Though there be no light that shines
You are Daylight intertwined

Nothing stops Your faithful Reign
Instilling Grace for needed change
Grandeur this Your gift of Peace
Ever nigh that swiftly meets

Gladly there You complete the heart
In Your work off the charts
Bringing a melody for Your redeemed
With Your lyrics given to sing

Every moment let eyes see
Endless Grace mushrooming
Wherever You lead feet to go
In starless moments to humbly know

Be still, and know…
Psalm 46:10

Then sings my soul…
-Carl Boberg, 1885

June 14

Before a word is on my tongue You, Lord, know it completely.
...even the darkness will not be dark to You; the night will shine
like the day, for darkness is as light to You.
Psalm 139:4, 12

Your quieting comforting care
Is unbelievably already there
Knowing each need of the broken
Before a word is even spoken

Like morning fog that surrounds
You are the clarity to be found
Nothing hinders nor dims Your light
Even in the darkest of long nights

Your Breath alone gives each soul
More than enough to be made whole
Looking upward to wholly see
Quieting comfort continually

How is it Lord that You graciously reveal
Steps of Grace for the brokenness we feel
See My Hands see My Feet
Each broken heart Mine came to complete

The Lord will guide you always; He will satisfy your needs in a
sun-scorched land and will strengthen your frame.
You will be like a well-watered garden,
like a spring whose waters never fail.
Isaiah 58:11

And He walks with me and He talks with me
And He tells me I am His own...
-Charles Austin Miles, 1912

June 15
Hope and Strength are gifts each day
For each breath without delay
Giver of ALL gave His only Son
Giving His ALL for everyone

Hope and Strength are given each day
By the Unseen in visible ways
To encourage each heart each step
Finding Rest where each are met

Hope and Strength His plan each day
In new mercies His giving way
Sometimes through the skies that declare
Sometimes through His Heart found there

Hope and Strength His plan this day
To be lived out not tucked away
Relying upon His Strength again
His treasury of Hope deep within

But those who hope in the Lord
will renew their strength.
They will soar on wings like eagles;
they will run and not grow weary,
they will walk and not be faint.
Isaiah 40:31

June 16

Hang on as the mighty winds blow
Hold on to the One Who enfolds
Find Rest in His mending there
As His Heart gives life altering care

He alone brings the breath of calm
Stilling inside though the storm rages on
He alone sustains within the winds
For hearts to see Grace His extends

Hang on as He brings breakthrough
Hold on as He speaks to You
Hear in the winds His gift His Will
Saying again: "Peace, be still"

Then He arose and rebuked the wind,
and said to the sea, "Peace, be still"
And the wind ceased and there was a great calm.
Mark 4:39

Though…
Yet will I rejoice…
The Sovereign Lord is my Strength.
Habakkuk 3:17-19

The winds and the waves shall obey Thy Will.
"Peace, be still!"
Whether the wrath of the storm-tossed sea,
Or struggles or evil, whatever it be,
No water can swallow the ship where lies
the Master of ocean and earth and skies:
They all shall sweetly obey Thy Will.
"Peace, be still! Peace, be still!"
They all shall sweetly obey Thy Will.
"Peace, Peace, be still!"
-Mary Baker, 1874

June 17
So then, God has granted even the Gentiles repentance unto life.
Acts 11:18

Again I come with tear-stained face
Within the metronome of Garden Grace
On each page of Your Word
Your chaperoning Heart is therein heard

There are no steps to be taken alone
Your Heartbeat is that metronome
That will not stop like Garden Grace
Where You will dry each tear-stained face

The Sovereign Lord will wipe away the tears from all faces.
Isaiah 25:8

June 18
Chosen before creation began
Providing the way all planned by Your Hand
That all would have forgiveness to be
In Your Presence eternally

Chosen yet the choice given to accept
To be Shepherd led and forever kept
You made the way but still give the choice
For each beloved lamb to hear and follow Your voice

Amazing Grace awaiting each soul
Provision in place that makes each whole
Amazing the ask is surrender within
To the One Who is the Beginning without end...

For HE chose us in HIM before the creation of the world
to be holy and blameless in HIS sight.
Ephesians 1:4

Amazing Grace how sweet the sound...
We've no less days to sing God's praise
than when we first begun...
-John Newton, 1779

June 19
Awakened to walk and breathe within
The day You created appointed again
To graciously see the beauty You send
That encircles each heart without end

The gift to wholly see and hear
To experience Your Heart unendingly near
Going with before and behind
In Your Light that illumines and shines

Directed to trust through uncertainties
Shepherded always so selflessly
Giving the Strength to carry on
Your Peace within immediately each dawn

The Lord is my Light and my Salvation…
Psalm 27:1

I love to tell the Story…
Of Jesus and His love…
-Kate Hankey, 1866

June 20
Neath the canopy of Your starlit Grace
Feeling summer's breeze upon my face
Serenaded by Your appointed song
Echoed out as morning calm

There intersecting sprinkles of Grace
Dew of Heaven felt on my face
Touches my heart in a sacred way
Living Water that strengthens each day

The dawning of such daily Grace
Your gift to behold through clouds that are faced
Reminding my heart You turn night to day
Lit by your Presence without delay

The coming toward of purposed Grace
Brings Hope within whatever is faced
The witness of outward change across the skies
Emboldens each step at every sunrise

The day is Yours, and Yours also the night;
You established the sun and moon. It was
You who set all the boundaries of the earth;
You made both summer and winter.
Psalm 74:16-17

Summer and winter, springtime and harvest
Sun moon and stars in their courses above
Join with all nature in manifold witness
To Thy great faithfulness, mercy and love

Pardon for sin, and a peace that endureth
Thine own dear Presence to cheer and to guide
Strength for today and bright hope for tomorrow
Blessings all mine with ten thousand beside!
-Thomas O. Chisholm, 1923

June 21
Each heartache we experience and feel
Is bathed in compassion You instill
Within each longing You reveal
Your Promised Presence that mends and heals

Each passage of time there to see
Your Heart intertwined miraculously
Always more intricate steps ahead
In Your steadfastness therein led

Each discouragement that is heard
Can find solace in Your Word
There to infuse Hope every day
Where lies dissolve and slither away

Each breath never alone
Each one fully known
Each appointed within time
Each to hear Love defined…

The Lord appeared to us in the past, saying:
"I have loved you with an everlasting love;
I have drawn you with unfailing kindness."
Jeremiah 31:3

Love Divine, all loves excelling
Joy of Heaven to earth come down…
Jesus, Thou art all compassion;
Pure unbounded, love Thou art…
-Charles Wesley, 1747

June 22
O my soul
Glory that flows
Joy within
Cradled by Him

O my eyes
This sunrise
Beauty beyond
Awakening dawn

O my King
That gladly brings
Recorded Grace
Unendingly placed

O my steps
Given to reflect
Unspoken how
Beauty of now

O my ears
Stilled to hear
His Heart Song
Whispering calm

O my soul
In ceaseless flow
Given again
Joy without end

The Joy of the Lord is my strength.
Nehemiah 8:10

June 23
You crown the year with Your goodness.
Psalm 65:11 NKJV

A smile You put upon my face
For heart-made beauty supplied by Grace
Refreshing the eyes given to behold
Majestic loveliness that never grows old

Into Your Goodness You invite
Seeing darkness turn to light
The miracle of change You daily bring
Renewing steps Calvary themed

Never a moment without You
Never a heartache You won't soothe
Never a fear that cannot be resolved
Never a problem that cannot be solved

Always an archway leading through
To rest in the knowledge of trusting You
You alone bore the crown for us
Proving Your Love for heart shaped dust

Nothing greater than laying down
At Your feet our entrusted crown
Giving thanks for Your perfect ways
Aforethought of Grace crowning all of our days

They lay their crowns before the throne and say:
"You are worthy, our Lord and God,
to receive glory and honor and power,
for You created all things, and by Your Will
they were created and have their being.
Revelation 4:10-11

June 24
Every day You alone declare
Faithfulness unendingly there
Giving eyes to graciously see
The endlessness of Your majesty

Every day You alone extend
Faithfulness without end
Purposed to strengthen hearts to know
Unendingness that won't let go

Every day You alone grant
Faithfulness You implant
Within each heart to wholly see
Your perfect ways unendingly

*Surely You have granted him unending blessings
and made him glad with the joy of Your Presence.
Psalm 21:6*

Take my moments and my days
Let them flow in endless praise…
-Frances Havergal, 1874

June 25
Today is already fully planned
Where each heart and feet will land
Into the path of mercy's view
Prepared in advance making all things new

Created to seek all that He gives
In His Word of Life then live
Grateful for each step and breath
Rest found in His faithfulness

Each day given graciously
Like new mercies continually
Each heart His alone will refresh
Within His gift of forgiveness…

Let the morning bring me word of Your unfailing love,
for I have put my trust in You.
Show me the way I should go,
for to You I lift up my soul.
Psalm 143:8

June 26
Never have I seen a sunray arch across the sky
Like a rainbow overhead before uplifted eyes
So amazing to see the rays on the west side
As brilliantly captured in the sunrise

Cloudless morning You supplied
For this moment to provide
Showing powerfully this day that You bring
Above and beyond Your Heart graced theme

Your artistry boldly on display
East to west like sins washed away
Everything furnished to the gravity held
Through the testimony of the torn veil

Nothing could stop Mercy's breakthrough
Overarching willingness outstretched by You
Giver of Grace over all time
Like today's testimony through Your sunshine

For as the heavens are high above the earth,
so great is His mercy toward those who fear Him;
as far as the east is from the west,
so far has He removed our transgressions from us.
Psalm 103:11-12

June 27
Direct my feet my hands my heart
As this day begins and starts
Into footprints that You will show
Leading through moments You already know

Direct my mind my thoughts my heart
To rest in Yours that lights the dark
Finding strength in Yours always there
Before a word is spoken in prayer

Direct my body my soul my heart
Within Your gracious bookended art
Going with before and behind
In perfect solace given through time

Direct my eyes my ears my heart
Uplifted listening through what Yours imparts
Forgiveness as mine written by Your Hand
Grace extended seen there in the sand

*But Jesus stooped down and began
writing on the ground with His finger.
John 8:6 AMP*

*May the Lord direct your hearts into the love of God
and into the steadfastness and patience of Christ.
2 Thessalonians 3:5 AMP*

June 28
How amazing each creature You made
And that You let Adam give each one its name
How each one is uniquely designed
By Your creativity therein assigned

Giving each one their rhythmic pace
Sometimes only seen by footprints placed
Some creatures for the night some for the day
But each one provided for in Your giving way

Yet further amazing each heart that You made
Anticipating the day to hear each call You by Name
How each one is given Grace to find
To be grafted into Your family line

Given intersecting footprints to see
Your Shepherding Heart faithfully
Ever Present night and day
Each heart provided for in Your giving way

Blessed are those whose Help is the God of Jacob,
whose Hope is in the Lord their God.
He is the Maker of heaven and earth, the sea, and
everything in them He remains faithful forever.
Psalm 146:5-6

Praise God from Whom all blessings flow
Praise Him, all creatures here below
Praise Him above ye heav'nly host.
Praise Father, Son and Holy Ghost.
-Thomas Ken, 1674

June 29
Help my heart deep inside
To acknowledge the goodness You provide
In the steps I would not choose
Trusting nothing is impossible with You

You quietly calm and still each fear
Reminding my heart that Yours is near
Never a breath appointed for naught
You said "It is finished" and then sins were bought

O Holy night brought surrendered change
From Heaven to earth to know Your Name
O Holiest of days that left nothing the same
Resurrected Hope that forever sustains

Reminder of undeniable Grace
Encircled within Your Vine's embrace
Helping my heart deep inside
To acknowledge the goodness You provide

I am the Vine; you are the branches.
If you remain in Me and I in you,
You will bear much fruit;
apart from Me you can do nothing.
John 15:5

June 30
Praise Him for another new day
Praise Him for His unending ways
Praise Him in the quiet before dawn
Praise Him for the path He places feet upon

Praise Him in the highest heavens above
Praise Him for His anchoring Love
Praise Him in the heights and depths
Praise Him through every single step

Praise Him awaking from or drifting to sleep
Praise Him for giving His rest and peace
Praise Him for ways He sees each through
Praise Him for being Faithful and True

On My Way Home

Praise the Lord.
Praise the Lord from the heavens;
Praise Him in the heights above.
Praise Him, sun and moon;
Praise Him all you shining stars.
Praise Him, you highest heavens
and you waters above the skies.
Praise the Lord.
Psalm 148:1, 3-4, 14b

All creatures of our God and King
Lift up your voice and with us sing
Alleluia! Alleluia!
Thou burning sun with golden beam,
Thou silver moon with softer gleam
O praise Him, O praise Him!
Alleluia! Alleluia!
-St. Francis of Assisi, 1225

Jane Spears

JULY

July 1

Another morning gloriously new
Another chapter written by You
Another moment to be still and know
Another gift of mercy's flow

The winds and waves they both obey
The quietness of calm immediate without delay
The echoed whispers of peace within
The nourishment of strength to believe again

We only grasp one moment at a time
To drink in such beauty purposefully designed
Step by step mile after mile
Accepting Your invitation to once again…smile

The Lord make His face shine on you and be gracious to you;
The Lord turn His face toward you and give you peace.
Numbers 6:25-26

Watching and waiting looking above
Filled with His goodness lost in His love…
This is my story this is my song
Praising my Savior all the day long…
-Fanny Crosby, 1873

July 2
Praise Him for His active Power
Visibly seen every hour
Praise Him for His surpassing greatness
Given through His unending faithfulness

Timber chosen for the greatest fall
Crushing with His heel His plan for all
Laying down His Power that day
For the fallen to live upright in His ways

No greater mercy to be found
Than His willing Heart He chose to lay down
To repair restore and redeem
Every heart by the Unseen

And as we someday see His Face
Held within His arms of Grace
One more time we will fall down
In gratefulness giving Him our crowns

Praise Him for His acts of power;
praise Him for His surpassing greatness.
Psalm 150:3

We Fall Down by Chris Tomlin, 1998

July 3
The very goal of Your Heart
Is to perfect unfinished art
With the Blood of Your Grace
Pivotal provision timed and placed

Giving what no debtor could pay
Forgiving sin You carried that day
Painting renewal by the washing away
Completing the goal of Your Heart on display

Your readable Word imprinted to see
Handwritten moments from Your gallery
The brush in Hand the chosen red
Daily became our hallowed Bread

Shelf-less beauty every day
Above and beyond in countless ways
Selfless Heart opening eyes once blind
Perfecting hearts through mercy's design

*He saved us not because of righteous things we had done
but because of His mercy. He saved us through
the washing of rebirth and renewal by the Holy Spirit.
Titus 3:5*

July 4
Thank You precious Morning Star
For Your nearness never far
Thank You precious saving Grace
For Your continual unhindered pace

Thank You precious Savior and King
For Your Song everlasting
Thank You precious Redeemer and Friend
For Your Peace You place within

My Peace I give you.
John 14:27

July 5

Thank You for giving life and breath
Thank You for giving feet their first steps
Thank You for giving each day ordained
Thank You for giving the lineage of change

Thank You for being life and breath
Thank You for holding each through each step
Thank You for creating this day ordained
Thank You for being the Hallelujah of change

The Lord is my Strength and my Song;
He has become my Salvation.
He is my God, and I will praise Him,
my father's God, and I will exalt Him.
Exodus 15:12

July 6
Waiting in trust lets a heart breathe again
Hoping in trust gives renewed strength within
Living in trust knows His unfailing care
Praying in trust echoes Peace already there

Growing in trust sees His seed graced with showers
Surrendering in trust finds direction He empowers
Listening in trust gives renewed ability to hear
Knowing in trust that He is unendingly near

*May the God of Hope fill you with all Joy and Peace
as you trust in Him, so that you may overflow
with Hope by the power of the Holy Spirit.
Romans 15:13*

July 7
Giver of morning Giver of Grace
Giver of quiet to wholly embrace
Giver of sight Giver of sound
Giver of Peace that wholly surrounds

Giver of steps Shepherd led
Giver of Truth to be wholly fed
Giver of Strength that felt each blow
Giver of Salvation to wholly know

Giver of breath from His alone
Giver of time to be wholly known
Giver of footprints there beside
Giver of comfort He wholly provides

Praise be to the God and Father of our Lord Jesus Christ,
the Father of compassion and the God of all comfort,
who comforts us in all our troubles, so that we can comfort those
in any trouble with the comfort we ourselves receive from God.
2 Corinthians 1:3-4

July 8

They were helped in fighting them…
because they cried out to Him during the battle.
He answered their prayers, because they trusted in Him.
…the battle was God's.
1 Chronicles 5:20, 22b

Thank You that there is nothing impossible for You to mend
To every detail Your Heart attends
Knowing the outcome of steps on their way
Within the time allotted You grant each day

O Granter of Hope Rest and Peace
For every trial You grant relief
Within the realm where Grace abounds
For every breath Your Heart is found

O Granter of Strength when the battle is fierce
O Living Hope that was willingly pierced
O Blood that flowed for every need
O Mercy Your gift that intercedes

Therefore He is able to save completely those who come to God
through Him, because He always lives to intercede for them.
Hebrews 7:25

July 9

Thank You for the moments You set in place
To see constancy of Your Heart as Grace
Through such faithfulness You open the Door
For all willing hearts to be known as Yours

Thank You for moments given to find
Your Heart alone as Love Divine
In Your Word still speaking today
For all to know Your Truth as Yahweh

The Son is the radiance of God's glory and the exact representation of His being, sustaining all things by His powerful Word. After He had provided purification for sins, He sat down at the right hand of the Majesty in heaven.
Hebrews 1:3

July 10
A daily template for all to see
Your creative Hand infinitely
In the faithful way that night takes a bow
When morning unfolds as You vowed

A daily imprint given to know
Your merciful Heart that loves each so
The Hands that surrendered for our "now"
Reviving our souls through Grace allowed

For you were once darkness, but now you are
light in the Lord. Live as children of light.
Ephesians 5:8

Now to the King eternal, immortal, invisible,
the only God, be honor and glory for ever and ever. Amen.
1 Timothy 1:17

July 11
Be still my soul like the clouds above
Find Rest my soul in His perfect love
Take time to listen in quietness
Within His unending faithfulness

Be still my soul at His guided pace
Find Rest my soul in His tour of Grace
Take time to breathe in the terrain of change
Umbrellaed beneath His Sovereign Reign

Be still my soul in steps each dawn
Find Rest my soul in keeping on
Take time to remember His promises made
He lovingly reveals in unclouded praise

*For Your faithfulness and lovingkindness are great,
reaching to the heavens, And Your truth to the clouds.
Be exalted above the heavens, O God;
Let Your glory and majesty be over all the earth.
Psalm 57:10-11 AMP*

O the land of cloudless day
O the land of an uncloudy day
-J. K. Alwood, 1885

July 12
Moving forward logistically
By Unseen footsteps unfalteringly
As You direct the sun from the east
So You lead and steady my feet

Moving forward methodically
By Unseen footsteps steadfastly
Into Grace steps leading the way
Hand held mercy with newness each day

Moving forward steadily
By Unseen footsteps readily
Faithfully held by outstretched Hand
Neath the shadow of Your Heart span

Moving forward rhythmically
By Unseen footsteps purposefully
Intentionally changed by Your sweat-drops
Never forsaken amid each hard spot

Moving forward assuredly
By Unseen footsteps lovingly
Unending renewal through mercy's dewdrops
Daily led by Your Heart my Rock

Whoever dwells in the shelter of the Most High
will rest in the shadow of the Almighty. I will say of the Lord,
"He is my refuge and my fortress, my God is Whom I trust."
Psalm 91:1-2

July 13

You give more than a heart can hold
You give more than eyes can behold
You give more than ears can contain
You give unendingly and remain

You give wonders You orchestrate
You give Salvation to celebrate
You give Mercy's endless view
You give reviving breath that renews

You give beyond the farthest star
You give reminders of how near You are
You give unhindered steps to take
You give surrender for each heart to make

You give Strength deep within
You give continually without end
You give Joy a place to dwell
You give Yourself as Emmanuel

Give thanks to the Lord, for He is good;
His love endures forever.
1 Chronicles 16:34

July 14
The crescent hung in the sky
Illumined smile to walk by
Faithful witness through the night
Until fading into morning light

The brilliance of the light that comes
To show that night is finished and done
Consuming movement leading the way
For purposed steps You illumine each day

No brighter fairer Light to shine
Than Grace-given Mercy within time
The revolutions You set in motion
Illumined by Your endless devotion

O Perfect Light for wayward steps
A Lamppost given that reflects
Your Way Home day and night
Illumined by your Heart and Might

Thank You for forming hearts to hold
Your Gift of Grace more precious than gold
And for the illumination of Your Heart to know
That changes from crimson to white as snow

*And there will no longer be any night;
and they will not have need of the light of a lamp
nor the light of the sun, because the Lord God
will illuminate them; and they will reign forever.
Revelation 22:5*

Silently now I wait for Thee,
Ready my God, Thy will to see
Open my eyes, illumine me,
Spirit divine!
-Clara H. Scott, 1895

July 15
Can I truly be forgiven once again
Yes My child I died for all of your sins
Can I truly receive unending Mercy and Grace
Yes My child I died to take your place

Can I truly live redeemed and free
Yes My child through My Blood on Calvary
Can I truly live in perfect Peace
Yes My child through My unending Strength

Can I truly be accepted and fully known
Yes My child I died for you as My own
Can I truly be comforted in my defeat
Yes My child I am your Mercyseat

Truly, truly, I say to you, whoever hears My Word and believes Him Who sent Me has eternal life. He does not come into judgment, but has passed from death to life.
John 5:24

Echoes of mercy, whispers of love…
Blessed Assurance by Fanny Crosby, 1873

July 16

Let me ponder Grace again
In this day deep within
Let me ponder wisdom's say
In this day from You, Yahweh

Let me ponder and discern
In this day desiring to learn
Let me ponder in the waiting
In this day without debating

Let me ponder steps to take
In this day before daybreak
Let me ponder listen and know
In this day to stop or go

*Ponder the path of your feet,
then all your ways will be sure.
Proverbs 4:26 ESV*

*Give careful thought to the paths for your
feet and be steadfast in all your ways.
Proverbs 4:26 NIV*

July 17
The silence of morning filled with calm
The heartbeat of dawn ambling on
Into places untouched and unmoved
Neath the wings that You choose

Gathered moments atop a tree
Outlook and outpost steadfastly
Watching faithfulness light up the sky
Neath the heights of heaven nearby

The intersection of this moment in time
From Your Heart that touches mine
Message clearly to be still and know
Neath Your unfailing Peaceful tempo

The eternal God is your refuge and dwelling place,
and underneath are the everlasting arms.
Deuteronomy 33:27 AMP

July 18
God of wonder and possibility
Who gives His Peace unendingly
God of comfort resoundingly
Who gave His Son astoundingly

*Now faith is confidence in what we hope for
and assurance about what we do not see.
Hebrews 11:1*

Nearer than my heart can imagine
Nearer than my mind can fathom
Nearer than my eyes can see
Nearer than my lungs can breathe

God of majesty sovereignly dwells
Who gives His Gift called Emmanuel
God of Grace like a waterfall
Who gave forgiveness once for all

Nearer than my soul can dwell
Nearer than my tongue can tell
Nearer than my life can be
Nearer than my breath is He

*The Lord is near.
Philippians 4:5*

Nearer, my God to Thee, nearer to Thee
E'en though it be a cross, That raiseth me
Still all my song shall be, Nearer, my God, to Thee;
Nearer, my God, to Thee, Nearer to Thee.
-Sarah F. Adams, 1840

July 19

Yet the Lord, the God of Israel, chose me from my whole family to be king over Israel forever. He chose Judah as leader, and from the tribe of Judah He chose my family, and from my father's sons He was pleased to make me king over all Israel.
1 Chronicles 28:4

The gift of being chosen David identified
Out of all of his brothers God had supplied
Yet he was chosen from shepherding
To someday be Israel's future king

Chosen not only by family but tribe
The one appointed to lead and guide
To rule within the chosen land
Promised for Israel as God had planned

We can be chosen and identified
By the Lamb that God alone supplied
Promised Messiah Shepherding King
Chosen by the Giver of everything

"Chosen" the vast honor God alone gives
Through Jesus His Son for all to live
In God's prepared chosen place
Heaven to dwell by choosing His Grace

But you are a chosen people, a royal priesthood, a holy nation, God's treasured possession, that you may declare the praises of Him who called you out of darkness into His wonderful light.
1 Peter 2:9

July 20
You, God, are my God, earnestly I seek You;
I thirst for You, my whole being longs for You,
in a dry and parched land where there is no water.
Psalm 63:1

Thank You for each hunger and thirst
That You alone satisfy on earth
Through Living Water and the Bread
Through each footstep Shepherd led

Thank You for each longing within
For Your Heart given that Grace extends
For higher ways and higher thoughts
Through each footstep Shepherd taught

Thank you for each hunger and thirst
For Your Power always at work
For Your Heart undivided
For each footstep Shepherd guided

Thank You for each longing within
For forgiveness that purifies from sin
For the price You paid and bought
For each footstep Shepherd sought

I sought the Lord, and He answered me;
He delivered me from all my fears.
Psalm 34:4

July 21

Only in quiet can a heart fully hear
Only in surrender can a heart feel You near
Only in trust can a heart truly move
Only in rest can a heart be renewed

Only in stillness can a heart fully know
Only in solace can a heart overflow
Only in release can a heart live unafraid
Only in Grace can a heart be remade

He only is my Rock and my Salvation;
He is my Defense; I shall not be moved.
Trust in Him at all times, you people,
pour out your heart before Him;
God is a Refuge for us. Selah
Psalm 62:6:8

Blessings as you walk within this day as His beloved…

July 22
Let my response grow to be
You are good in what is before me
Let my eyes upwardly see
You are good unendingly

Let my heart find rest believing
You are good and never leaving
Let my soul holdfast and recall
You are good and Lord of all

May Your saints rejoice in Your goodness.
2 Chronicles 7:41

God Of All by Twila Paris, 2003

July 23
See the woman at the well
Coming empty with her pail
See her turbulent waters there
Empty living in longing despair

Jesus loves her this we know
For He stopped to tell her so
She needed more than her pail could hold
And there was chosen to see His Heart of gold

Demonstrating to this beloved broken daughter
His eternal quenching Living Water
That flowed not from Abraham's well
But through the veins of Emmanuel

*Whoever believes in Me, as Scripture has said,
rivers of living water will flow from within them.
John 7:38*

There is a fountain filled with blood
Drawn from Immanuel's veins
And sinners, plunged beneath that flood,
Lose all their guilty stains
-William Cowper, 1772

July 24
You know the number of steps on the trail
You know the pearls still hidden in shells
You know the endurance for each mountain to climb
You know the wrestling and the strength each will find

You know the "Thank You" that will be said
You know the footprints that will become Grace led
You know the dawn before it breaks
You know the soul before each one awakes

You know the Song each desires to hear
You know the whisper soon placed in each ear
You know the timing before it takes place
You know the moments each heart will embrace

You know the morning laden with dew
You know the catalyst that makes all things new
You know the way each seed is sown
You know the timing when Peace will be known

You know when I sit down and when I get up.
· You know my thoughts from far away.
You know where I go and where I lie down.
You know everything I do.
Lord, You know what I want to say
even before the words leave my mouth.
You are all around me in front of me and behind me.
I feel Your Hand on my shoulder.
I am amazed at what You know;
it is too much for me to understand.
Psalm 139:2-6 ERV

July 25
From the rising of the dawn
There's a path to walk upon
Winding through this very day
In Your covering that's Heartmade

Shining light to wholly see
Declared handiwork perfectly
Filling the skies hearts and minds
To give praise for Your design

Poured out Mercy like Your Grace
Already in motion taken place
To know strength and rest within
As each day of renewal begins

In Your covering that's Heartmade
In Your Word that You gave
There's a path to walk upon
Neath Your faithfulness each dawn

Let the Name of the Lord be praised,
both now and forevermore.
From the rising of the sun to the place where it sets,
the Name of the Lord is to be praised.
Psalm 113:2-3

July 26
Unchanging God that fills the skies
With quiet clouds that float by
That form the eyes to behold
Your daily Grace as it unfolds

Unchanging God that fills the earth
With the grandeur of Your work
Tirelessly awaiting to impart
Daily Grace to more hearts

Unchanging God that fills my soul
That heals what's broken and makes whole
With Hands that formed a place inside
To be my Grace You daily provide

*But You remain the same,
and Your years will never end.
Psalm 102:27*

July 27
Why do I miss them so much today
Memories made heart-tucked away
Almost the anniversary of their wedding day
Where unending love was given to stay

Thank You for the example to be
Living beside one's beloved faithfully
For seeing through life's ups and downs
Your unending faithfulness that wholly surrounds

You were there for their every step
As they taught mine own were kept
In Your Word that never fails
Because of one moment of the torn veil

Thank You for Your Grace every day
That is present and heart-tucked away
When perfect Love was forever made known
The anniversary of finding the Way Home

For the Lord had given them cause to rejoice…
2 Chronicles 20:27

How beautiful are the feet of those who bring good news.
Romans 10:15

So then faith comes from hearing
and hearing from the Word of God.
Romans 10:17

(In loving memory of my beloved parents
who faithfully taught me the way Home…)

July 28
As I lay me down You bless
Giving me Your perfect Rest
Teaching that ceasing is a gift
From Your Heart from Your lips

Teach me first my need to rest
Listening assuredly to what is next
Trusting in each step You make
Will be the path You give to take

*You will keep in perfect peace those whose minds
are steadfast, because they trust in You.
Trust in the Lord forever, for the Lord,
the Lord Himself is the Rock eternal.
Isaiah 26:3-4*

July 29

Lead my steps take me where
You have already graciously prepared
Lead my heart in ways unknown
You have already removed the stone

Lead my eyes to openly see
You have already lived perfectly
Lead my ears to wholly hear
You have already spoken clear

Lead my soul to trustingly know
You have already paved the road
Lead my thoughts to firmly believe
You have already provided for each need

Hear my cry, O God; attend unto my prayer.
From the end of the earth will I cry unto Thee,
when my heart is overwhelmed;
lead me to the Rock that is higher than I.
Psalm 61:1-2 KJV

July 30
Time alone spent with You
Helps my soul live renewed
In a way I could not otherwise know
The precious kindness You bestow

Time alone is given to see
Everything flows unendingly
Through Your willing nail-pierced Hands
For every heart to know Your plan

Time alone is where to find
The treasure trove You left behind
Footprints leading not just to a place
But into the timelessness of forgiving Grace

Be still and know…
Psalm 46:10

I come to the garden alone
While the dew is still…
-C. Austin Miles, 1913

July 31
Where is the Rest that You bring
In My quiet whispering
Where is the Strength that You provide
In My stillness given inside

Where is the Peace that You supply
In My words before I died
Where is the Joy in the pain
In My Heart that brings yours change

Where is the Calm as the storm rages on
In My faithfulness visible each dawn
Where is the Treasure given to find
In My Grace sufficient through time

Where is the Forgiveness to be known
In My Compassion already shown
Where is the Life the Truth and the Way
In My Presence with you each day

And lo, I am with you always.
Matthew 28:20 KJV

AUGUST

August 1
Dedication to His garden
Blessings abundant through His pardon
Watered by His Might each hour
Producing Hope through unrivaled Power

His bouquet of forget-me-nots
A Grace reminder that never stops
Always with before and behind
No greater message for heart soul and mind

Never alone and never will be
Always with through Calvary
What gracious Grace and endless flow
That will not cease for all to know…

*May the God of Hope fill you
with all joy and peace as you trust in Him,
so that you may overflow with Hope
by the power of the Holy Spirit.
Romans 15:13*

August 2

Let my heart quickly hear
Your Heart beating ever near
Let my words slowly come
Remembering first Your Will be done

Let my longing patiently be shown
Your answers are timed by Grace alone
Let my waiting visibly become
Nothing less than Your victory won

Let my scars trustingly reveal
Grace unending that restores and heals
Let my joy heartily flow
Through the reclamation the Cross bestows

Let my heart willingly show
Yours alone like a straight arrow
Let my words openly confess
Immeasurable ways of Your faithfulness

*That My joy may remain in you,
and that your joy may be full.
John 15:11 NKJV*

O Love that will not let me go
I rest my weary soul in Thee
I give Thee back the life I owe
That in Thine ocean depths its flow
may richer fuller be
-George Matheson, 1882

August 3
Ever the bright and Morning Star
Ever-Present that's Who You are
Ever the Light showing the way
Ever Emmanuel each night each day

Ever leading the way Home
Ever reflecting faithfulness shown
Ever revealing Your finishing touch
Ever merciful and more than enough

For Your Love is ever before me,
and I walk continually in Your Truth.
Psalm 26:3

The Lord is my Light and my Salvation.
Psalm 27:1

August 4
Thank You that You moved the heart of Cyrus
Thank You that You healed the daughter of Jairus
Thank You that You resurrected Lazarus
Thank You that You redeemed through Jesus

Thank You that You still move hearts today
Thank You that You still heal daughters of clay
Thank You that You still resurrect Your beloved known
Thank You that still redeem through Christ alone

Jesus said to her, "I am the Resurrection and the Life. The one who believes in Me will live, even though they die; and whoever lives by believing in Me will never die. Do you believe this?"
John 11:25-26

August 5
Waiting is watching His timing take place
Waiting is believing His Sufficient Grace
Waiting is responding to His responsive ways
Waiting is resting in His Peace each day

Waiting is yielding to His plan
Waiting is surrendering into His Hands
Waiting is trusting His measured length
Waiting is relying upon His daily Strength

Waiting is honoring His rightful place
Waiting is agreeing with His pace
Waiting is acknowledging His sovereignty
Waiting is choosing His melody

Wait for the Lord,
be strong and take heart
and wait for the Lord.
Psalm 27:14

Then sings my soul…

August 6

There is Faith awaiting hearts to ask
There is Faith given hearts to grasp
There is Faith provision from the Lamb
There is Faith given by the Great I AM

There is Hope waiting to be received
There is Hope given for every single need
There is Hope to carry out His plan
There is Hope given in His outstretched Hand

There is Love more capable than ever
There is Love given that will never be severed
There is Love that reaches out longingly
There is Love given to indwell unendingly

*There is no greater love
than to lay down one's life for one's friends.
John 15:13 NLT*

*This is My commandment:
Love each other in the same way I have loved you.
John 15:12 NLT*

*And now these three remain: faith, hope and love.
But the greatest of these is love.
1 Corinthians 13:13*

August 7
Great God of Peace and Strength within
How amazing You give again and again
As we struggle grasping provision
Teach us the gift of Your wisdom

You already provide what matters most
The gift of Grace that is forever not almost
The security You designed hearts to know
Through unending mercies abundant not slow…

Now may the Lord of peace Himself
give you peace at all times and in every way.
The Lord be with all of you.
2 Thessalonians 3:16

August 8

You are my Hope given to know
You are my Help given to grow
You are my Strength given to believe
You are my Peace given to breathe

You are my Song given to sing
You are my Rest given to cling
You are my Shepherd given to lead
You are my Calm given to receive

You are my Forgiveness given to heal
You are my Grace given to instill
You are my Steadfastness given to endure
You are my Provision given to assure

The steadfast love of the Lord never ceases;
His mercies never come to an end;
they are new every morning;
great is Your faithfulness.
Lamentations 3:22-23 ESV

August 9
You intervened in Joseph's dreams
Teaching Your timing for future scenes
You intervened at the Red Sea
Teaching nothing is impossible for Thee

You intervened through the wilderness
Teaching Your provision of faithfulness
You intervened through the Jordan River
Teaching Your power is able to deliver

You intervened through walls that crumbled
Teaching Your plan is given to humble
You intervened through hearts every day
Teaching Rest was found only in Yahweh

*Since You are my Rock and my Fortress,
for the sake of Your Name lead and guide me.
Psalm 31:3*

A Mighty Fortress is our God
A bulwark never failing…
-Martin Luther, 1529

August 10

Stops we make along the way
Are meant to see what He conveys
On the path that He designed
Repeated faithfulness every time

Stops allow a change of pace
For hearts to see His visible Grace
Open to experience unexpected delight
Shown precisely day or night

Stops are temporary like clouds allowed
Housed within His Shelter of now
Carefully quieting and stilling steps
To know His permanence through what is next…

He leads me beside the still waters…
Psalm 23:2 NKJV

August 11

In the shadows there beside
Is Your Hand to lead and guide
In the moments when dark surrounds
Is Your Light given to be found

In uncertainty the day may hold
Is Your Hand that never lets go
In winds that change the trajectory
Is Your Peace unendingly

In steps given there to take
Is Yours that will never forsake
In night shifting into dawn
Is Your whisper to keep pressing on…

Press on…
Philippians 3:14

And we know [with great confidence] that God [who is deeply concerned about us] causes all things to work together [as a plan] for good for those who love God, to those who are called according to His plan and purpose.
Romans 8:28 AMP

I'm pressing on the upward way…
Lord plant my feet on higher ground
Johnson Oatman, Jr., 1898

August 12

He made the moon to mark the seasons,
and the sun knows when to go down.
Psalm 104:19

Thank You for Your promises to stand upon
To be comforted by every dawn
Thank You that they will never fail
And that Your authored Hope timelessly prevails

Thank You that each promise is not built for a shelf
But is interactive comfort given from Yourself
To be held forever in heart and hand
To be worn like pages read as planned

Hold our hearts as we hold onto
Every promise given by You
To know in part but lived in full
In Your forgiveness as Your Grace-schooled

Now I know in part;
then I shall know fully, even as I am fully known.
1 Corinthians 13:12

August 13
*But I prayed, Now strengthen my hands.
Nehemiah 6:9*

Now strengthen my hands to do the work
Appointed for me upon the earth
Now strengthen my feet to move at the pace
Purpose filled in steps of Grace

Now strengthen my eyes to wholly see
Your plan unfolding entrusted to me
Now strengthen my ears to listen each day
Hearing Your instruction and augustly obey

Now strengthen my heart surrendered unto
In wholehearted direction that glorifies You
Now strengthen the way of Truth to walk
Willing through Rest that does not stop

*For we are God's handiwork,
created in Christ Jesus to do good works,
which God prepared in advance for us to do.
Ephesians 2:10*

August 14
There's a daily pace
In the cadence of Grace
There's a continual flow
In this Rest to know

There's a Hand to hold
In this Grace that enfolds
There's a path to take
In this Rest that He makes

There's a momentum divine
In this Grace for the finish line
There's a motion designed
In this Rest governing time

There's a movement of steps
In this Grace that protects
There's a dance deep within
In this Rest copyrighted by Him

*But He said to me, "My Grace is sufficient for you,
for My power is made perfect in weakness."
Therefore I will boast all the more gladly about my
weaknesses, so that Christ's power may Rest on me.
2 Corinthians 12:9*

August 15
Thank You for the timing of Your Grace
Given for each moment set in place
Nothing to be experienced or ever faced
Without the comfort of Your endless embrace

Thank You for the timing of Peace You instill
That there are no moments overpowering Your Will
No emptiness impossible for You to fill
No hurt impossible You cannot heal

Thank You for the timing given just now
For this very moment clouds allowed
Reminding my heart deep within
That soon they will hold Your appearance again

Thank You for the timing You spent right here
So all could believe You are forever near
And that the answers each seek to find
Was given through Mercy that outlasts time

I will bless the Lord at all times;
His praise will continually be in my mouth.
Psalm 34:1 AMP

August 16
Come the kindest word spoken
For the hurting wounded and broken
Come finding a Savior there
The very Answer to whispered prayer

Come is an invitation to walk
For every turn for every stop
Come is the quiet He gives within
Unraveling the stresses when shared with Him

Come to be restored and renewed
In His wonders of how He moves
Come to know His soothing song
Of every note "to Him belong"

Come to Me,
all who are weary and burdened
and I will give you rest.
Matthew 11:28

Jesus loves me this I know
For the Bible tells me so
Little ones "to Him belong"…
-Anna B. Warner, 1859

August 17
God of Mercy that lets eyes see
Faithfulness present relentlessly
God of Grandeur that lets hearts know
Faithfulness present as a continual flow

God of Peace that calms the waves
Faithfulness present every day
God of Grace that is never routine
Faithfulness present amid every scene

God of Impossible authoring Truth
Faithfulness present through Boaz and Ruth
God of Footprints leading the way
Faithfulness present now and always

God of Comfort to hurting souls
Faithfulness present there to console
God of Victory already won
Faithfulness present shown through Your Son

For great is Your love, reaching to the heavens;
Your faithfulness reaches to the skies.
Be exalted, O God, above the heavens;
let Your glory be over all the earth.
Psalm 57:10-11

August 18
Let each step I dare to take
Follow the ones Your footprints make
Leading into each new day
Quieted by each word You say

Reminding my eyes through the dark
That You are the Keeper of my heart
Already there to hold my hand
Light pouring forth as You planned

Beckoning in the silence to hear
An inward place to draw near
Where darkness may surely surround
But in the center Light is found

You equip You prepare
For my heart to live aware
Of Your inextinguishable Light
Ever attentive through the night

Thank You for Your Lamplight there
Reminding my heart of Your personalized care
Thank You that Your knowable pace
Illumines each step with light-giving Grace

Your Word is like a lamp that guides my steps,
a light that shows the path I should take.
Psalm 119:105 ERV

August 19
Thank You for Your resounding echoing Grace
Encouraging each dawn to continue the race
Thank You for Your unending pace
Intended to end in Your embrace

Thank You for Your changeless Truth
Housed within Your holy pursuit
Thank You for Your eternal Rest
Sacrificially Your holy quest

Thank You for Your Grace that instills
Righteousness that covers and heals
Thank You for Your mercy shown
Tabernacled to be fully known

Shouts of joy and victory resound in the tents of the righteous;
"The Lord's right hand has done mighty things!"
Psalm 118:15

August 20
You are the Beginning that has no end
You are the Gardener that sovereignly tends
You are our Rest deep inside
You are our Giver that endlessly provides

You are our Grace that is always more than
You are Yahweh of possible and can
You are the Word needed each day
You are the Wisdom available always

You are our Mercy calming within
You are the Forgiver of every sin
You are the Truth to be told
You are the Life to behold

You are our Hope that surrounds
You are our Peace to be found
You are the Glory to worship each day
You are our Hallelujah now and always

*Our Father which art in Heaven,
hallowed be Thy Name.*
Matthew 6:9

August 21
Each place I have been You were there
Each place I am You are my Watch-care
Each place I will be You will be
Each place beside faithfully

No place have I struggled without Your Hand
No place am I without Your Strength to stand
No place will I be without Your Face
No place without Your faithful Grace

Every time I stop to reminisce
There I see Your faithfulness
Interwoven through threads of Grace
By the One that took my place

*O Lord, God of Israel, there is no God like You
in heaven above or on earth below…
1 Kings 8:23*

August 22
You remembered us on Your hardest day
That Your sacrifice was the only way
Reconciliation could possibly be made
Through Your Blood given to save

You remembered us on Your walk toward Calvary
That Your sacrifice would redirect steps eternally
Reconciliation that would once and for all make whole
Through Your Forgiveness for every soul

You remembered us in spite of the pain
Setting Your Heart on the Joy of the gain
Reconciliation would be the greatest gift received
Through every heart accepting You for every need

You remembered us so we could know
The unending Mercy from Heaven's flow
Reconciliation You alone made possible
Through Your Word our forever Gospel

He knows how we were formed,
He remembers we are dust.
Psalm 103:14

And He took bread, gave thanks and broke it,
and gave it to them, saying, "This is My Body
which is for you; do this in remembrance of Me."
Luke 22:19

August 23

Through the watches of the night
Comes the promise of faithful light
Likened to Hope given to shine
Through the darkness known in time

Through the watches of the day
Synchronized Hope leads the way
Into the steps given to shine
His reflection in this gift of time

Through the watches around the clock
Faithfulness will never stop
He gave His Heart to permanently shine
Through His forgiveness known throughout time

Through the watch care deep within
There is Grace given to mend
Then His image begins to shine
Within His vessel held through all time

Through the watch care of uneven terrain
Through each step His sustains
Through His vastness unhindered to shine
Through His Heart placed within time

You, Lord, keep my lamp burning;
my God turns my darkness into light.
Psalm 18:28

When Jesus spoke again to the people, He said, "I am the light of the world. Whoever follows Me will never walk in darkness, but will have the light of the life."
John 8:13

August 24
We are cleansed and clothed
By His love fully known
We are redeemed and seen
By His Blood as the means

We are covered and bought
By His Word we are taught
We are pardoned and whole
By His Grace this we know

We are healed and blessed
By His affirming Rest
We are held and treasured
By His Mercy beyond measure

*Now to Him
who is able
to do immeasurably more
than all we ask or imagine,
according to His power
that is at work within us,
to Him be glory
in the church
and in Christ
Jesus throughout
all generations,
for ever and ever!
Ephesians 3:20-21*

August 25

Hard moments that came let me see in a different way
That You alone are in control of every day
And that there is always more ahead
For hearts that believe every Word You have said

So I breathe amazed by what has taken place
Looking back seeing only Your faithful Grace
In ways that I otherwise would never have grown
If not for those hard places that were inwardly sown

Thank You for fire, for water, for wind
That You recorded where your footprints have been
In each experience written down
Your Presence was there boots on the ground

Thank You that we are never alone
In the hard moments each have known
And that the realness of knowing this proof
Is found in Your Word of unending Truth

But this is what you must do:
Tell the Truth to each other.
Zechariah 8:16

Jesus said to him, "I am the [only] Way
[to God] and the [real] Truth and the [real] Life;
No one comes to the Father but through Me."
John 14:6 AMP

Glory! Glory! Hallelujah
Glory! Glory! Hallelujah
His Truth is marching on
-Julia Ward Howe, 1862

August 26
He has caused His wonders to be remembered;
the Lord is gracious and compassionate.
Psalm 111:4

The fear of the Lord is the beginning of wisdom;
all who follow His precepts have good understanding.
To Him belongs eternal praise.
Psalm 111:10

Mom ended her letters with this phrase
"In God's eternal love and praise"
Reading the reference her eyes saw
And how she pointed to Christ her all in all

Thankful as my heart read these words
That meant so much also to hers
That she would end each letter this way
Giving glory and honor to God always

Lord, You have been our dwelling place throughout all
generations.
Before the mountains were born or You brought forth the whole
world,
from everlasting to everlasting You are God.
Psalm 90:1-2

August 27

I will give you Rest as sure as the stars
I will give you Rest wherever you are
I will give you Rest perfectly timed
I will give you Rest My Grace designed

I will be your Rest for heart soul and mind
I will be your Rest your Treasure to find
I will be your Rest that wholly refines
I will be your Rest because you are Mine

Come to Me,
all you who are weary and burdened,
and
I will give you rest.
Matthew 11:28

Because You are my Help,
I sing in the shadow of Your wings.
I cling to You;
Your right Hand upholds me.
Psalm 63:7-8

August 28
Morning is my favorite time
In the solitude of quiet rhyme
Listening hearing receiving more
From Your Heart that daily restores

Morning given to reawaken into
Steps that You will walk me through
To behold firsthand such Grace
In Your created learning space

Morning extinguishing the dark of night
Tenderly given Your spoken Light
Recorded there to read and see
Faithfulness beyond degree

Morning is directed and empowered
By Your Goodness the hungry devour
Retelling the fulfillment in Your daily way
"Let there be light" as long as it is day

Morning comes always on time
Fashioned intentionally by design
To drink in beauty and breathless be
Within Your creation for hearts to see

*And God said, "Let there be light," and there was light.
God saw that the light was good, and He separated
the light from the darkness. God called the light "day,"
and the darkness He called "night." And there was evening,
and there was morning—the first day.
Genesis 1:3-5*

August 29
Where You lead let me move
Where You guide let me choose
Where You provide let me rely
Where You bless let me profess

Because…
Faithful You are Faithful You'll be
Faithful You are eternally
Faithful You are Faithful today
Faithful You are in every way

Where You bring let me cling
Where You direct let me sing
Where You sustain let me reside
Where You instill let me abide

Because…
Faithful You are Faithful again
Faithful You are each breath within
Faithful You are Faithful You've been
Faithful You are forever Amen

*The Lord is faithful to all His promises
and loving toward all He has made.
Psalm 145:13*

August 30
Good morning His Heart says each day
Across the skies in His giving ways
Through each color on display
From the same Potter that formed the clay

Good morning His Heart quiets and stills
Through His Word His Truth reveals
Ricocheted Grace the heavens instill
Beauty through knees that surrendered His Will

Good morning by His speech designed
His same breath that became yours and mine
Not just within the perimeter of time
But by Resurrected Breath our eternal lifeline

*Then the Lord God formed a man from the dust of the ground
and breathed into his nostrils the breath of life,
and the man became a living being.
Genesis 2:7*

August 31

You prepared Light spoken to glow
You prepared Mercy meant to know
You prepared each breath to take
You prepared forgiveness for each mistake

You prepared kindness in every step
You prepared mindfulness in being met
You prepared layers of evergreen
You prepared Grace for every scene

You prepared moments to fully hear
You prepared heartbeats to feel Yours near
You prepared unraveling to be made new
You prepared Hope to be the dream come true

Christ Jesus our Hope.
1 Timothy 1:1

For we are God's handiwork, created in
Christ Jesus to do good works, which
God prepared in advance for us to do.
Ephesians 2:10

SEPTEMBER

September 1
The worn pages of Your Word
Touching hearts in what is heard
Promises You alone fulfill
Word made flesh as surrendered Will

The very Holiness held each day
As hands hold onto what You say
Receiving life abundant without delay
Written to read and believe always

No other book here on earth
Holds the Hope of Your unending work
Finished through Your only Son
Through arms outstretched for everyone

From cover to cover on every page
You alone are center stage
Redemption revealed as You planned
Through Grace built on the Rock to stand

*Let us hold unswervingly to the Hope we profess,
for He who promised is faithful.
Hebrews 10:23*

September 2
Foreshadowing light
The Red Sea plight
Foreshadowing rays
That paved the way

Foreshadowing Grace
Each trial faced
Foreshadowing Redemption
Through Divine intervention

Foreshadowing meal
Communion revealed
Foreshadowing peace
Poured out to drink

Foreshadowing atonement
Intersected moment
Foreshadowing Heaven
Risen without leaven

Foreshadowing sacred
Through the wayward
Foreshadowing Rest
Through Faithfulness

*Such things are only a shadow of what is to come
and they have only symbolic value; but the substance
[the reality of what is foreshadowed] belongs to Christ.
Colossians 2:17 AMP*

September 3

What a gift that You bring the rain
A bountiful blessing of needed change
What a great Mercy to unendingly know
Quieted Rest even in the shadows

What a gift You touch each heart
In refreshing newness You alone impart
What a great Mercy like morning dew
In the forgiveness borne through You

What a gift You forever remain
Interceding for our needed change
What a great Mercy that all can know
Rest neath the wing of Your shadow

*Whoever dwells in the shelter of the Most High
will rest in the shadow of the Almighty.
Psalm 91:1*

Still
-Rueben Morgan, 2002

September 4
Guiding our hearts and wayward feet
Guiding us Home to His Mercyseat
Guiding us always by day and night
Guiding us powerfully like the Israelites

Guiding through the wilderness
Guiding through our brokenness
Guiding through unparalleled battles faced
Guiding through unrivaled Wisdom and Grace

Guiding safely by exact known steps
Guiding where we are mercifully met
Guiding faithfully no matter the need
Guiding always each who believes…

For this God is our God for ever and ever;
He will be our Guide even to the end.
Psalm 48:14

Guide me, O Thou Great Jehovah,
Pilgrim through this barren land;
I am weak, but Thou art Mighty,
Hold me with Thy powerful Hand.
Bread of Heaven, Bread of Heaven,
Feed me till I want no more;
Feed me till I want no more.
-William Williams, 1745

September 5
Arise and prepare to behold
What I planned for your heart to hold
Another sunrise I'll place in the sky
Cannot wait to see the joy in your eyes

Together we can enjoy what I create
There I stand opening the morning gate
Waiting for you to come gaze again
Upon appointed beauty I place within

Not just the sight but also the sound
Of your heart walking this sacred ground
Where the slate of the day is mercifully clean
And added joy fills the unfolding scenes

So come to enjoy this "breaking of bread"
This fellowship time where you are Shepherd led
Finding again always more than enough
Of ways you can know My unending touch

Count your blessings name them every one
Count your blessings morning has come
Count your blessings as fast as dragonflies
Count your blessings that outlasts each sunrise

Light is sweet, and it pleases the eye to see the sun.
Ecclesiastes 11:7

O Lord,
in the morning will I direct my prayer
unto Thee, and will look up.
Psalm 5:3 KJV

September 6
There is not an empty place
That is not filled with Your Grace
You fill the Heavens not just a room
You are the miracle within the seedling's bloom

There is not a single place
That is able to vacate Your Grace
You created everything we see and hear
You give each lung its breath and years

There is not a possible place
That is independent of your Grace
For You were before and will always be
Between and beside every happening

There is not a better place
Than being forgiven housing Your Grace
Knowing your purposed Will as done
Resting assured where Light has come

Arise, shine, for your light has come,
and the glory of the Lord rises upon you.
Isaiah 60:1

September 7
Renew a steadfast spirit within
Sustained by Your Spirit without end
Restore the Joy of Your Salvation
Borne through Grace without reservation

Remind my heart each day each step
Of Your faithfulness that intersects
Hearing hearts seeing eyes
With purposed Hope in each sunrise

And that You are the Anchor that holds
Lives together to behold
Unfailing Love endlessly
Reassurance continuously

Through the Cross then empty grave
Selfless Gift that You gave
Planned in advance for Your Kingdom come
Forgiven footprints as Your Will be done

Create in me a clean heart, O God;
and renew a right spirit within me.
Psalm 51:10 KJV

September 8
Stillness is a rhythmic pace
Settling within quieted Grace
A place of refuge housing relief
Hearing His Heartbeat giving His strength

Stillness is already prepared
To hear the whispered Hope intentionally there
Encouragement to embrace each day
Through such tenderness leading the way

Stillness brings the gift of calm
Resting in His soothing Psalm
Spoken deep within to know
Peace from the Maker of every soul

Stillness remains a garden choice
Finding solace in His voice
Acknowledging His wisdom opens heart eyes
Solely through Mercy His Heart provides

Thank You for the answers only You can give
Teaching us to trust as our way to live
Thank You for knowing all things ahead of time
Teaching us to trust Your purpose and design

Thank You for the outcomes You already know
Teaching that no matter what You never will let go
Thank You for the changes only You can bring
Teaching us to remember our part is thanksgiving

*The Lord gives strength to His people;
the Lord blesses His people with peace.
Psalm 29:11*

This is my story this is my song
Praising my Savior all the day long
-Fanny Crosby, 1873

September 9
The heart beneath the moon before the rains
The clouds in the wind bringing the respite of change
The moonlight You set for this moment to see
Was a gift touching my heart so deeply

For I know You are the Director that directs
The Protector that protects
The Instructor that instructs
The Constructor that constructs

Moments that we could otherwise miss
If eyes didn't look to the heavens like this
To see a moment revealed for simply then
That You placed precisely with the cloud in the wind

He makes clouds rise from the ends of the earth;
He sends lightning with the rain and
brings out the wind from His storehouses.
Psalm 135:7

September 10

You alone are my Help through pain
You alone are the One Who sustains
You alone give Your strength to stand
You alone lead me by Your Hand

You uphold when my heart is weary
You uphold in my moments that are teary
You uphold against all odds
You uphold and alone are God

You enfold by Your Grace alone
You enfold by Your Mercy shown
You enfold by Your Peace within
You enfold by Your Faithfulness without end

I love you, Lord, my strength.
The Lord is my rock, my fortress and my deliverer;
my God is my rock, in whom I take refuge...
In my distress I called to the Lord;
I cried to my God for help.
From His temple He heard my voice;
my cry came before Him, into His ears.
Psalm 18:1-2, 6

September 11

Changeless God changeless ways
Everlastingly throughout always
Changing souls to changelessness
By Your Grace and Holiness

Sustaining Hope sustaining Stay
Everlastingly throughout all days
Changing hopelessness to Hope within
Restful Strength given without end

God of Glory God of Might
God of Salvation changing darkness to Light
God of Deliverance to wandering feet
God of Grace that forgives and completes

The people walking in darkness have seen a great light; on those living in the land of the shadow of death a light has dawned.
Isaiah 9:2

Cast your cares on the Lord and He will sustain you.
Psalm 55:22

September 12
Hope surrounds as His theme
Fulfillment of His Father's dream
Coming giving breath and life
Fulfillment through His sacrifice

Hope beckons every day
Encouraging each heart along the way
Believing unending life anew
Has come for each heart His dream come true

Hope is waiting to ultimately see
The One Who loves so completely
Mending reconciling making a way
To abide in Him every single day

Hope is His faithful gift always
From the Heart of His Father, Yahweh
Who willingly came to do the finished work
To fulfill His Father's dream of heart rebirth

Every promise has been fulfilled; not one has failed.
Joshua 23:14

When God fulfills your longings, sweetness fills your soul.
Proverbs 13:19 TPT

September 13

You made the quiet morning dew
That points each heart to receive mercies new
You are the Giver giving again
More than hearts can even take in

So much abundance You made increments of days
To celebrate humbly Your giving ways
Daily giving shepherded purpose to move
Into the pattern of receiving from You

Teaching that every single breath
Is given for hearts to find restful rest
Trusting and knowing each heartbeat alone
Is given to hear Yours forever as known

My Presence will go with you and I will give you rest.
Exodus 33:14

There is a place of quiet rest
Near to the Heart of God…
-Cleland B. McAfee, 1903

September 14
Time we are given to listen and learn
To grow in wisdom and discern
To hear the Word recorded each day
That instruct to walk in His ways

Time we are given a gift unearned
To grow deeper in holy concerns
To hear His Heart in every step
That lead and guide and His reflect

Time we are given to fully know
The One Who came to love us so
To hear each dawn to walk within
The footprints left that lead to Him

Blessed are those who have learned to acclaim You, who walk in the light of Your Presence, O Lord.
Psalm 89:15

And He walks with me
And He talks with me
And He tells me I am His own…
-In The Garden by C. Austin Miles, 1913

September 15

Thank You for the words You will convey
Within my heart here today
To be still again and know
Your faithfulness that overflows

Touching the deepest part of me
Changing my heart continually
Into the vessel You wholly see
Through Jesus Blood on Calvary

The forgiven stance that You give
Teaching my heart to truly live
Freely in unending Grace
Every day as morning breaks

O my Strength, I watch for You;
You, O God, are my Fortress, my loving God.
Psalm 59:9

O my Strength, I sing praise to You;
You, O God are my Fortress, my loving God.
Psalm 59:17

September 16
In my distractions still my thoughts
Tender my heart as one being taught
Teach my soul to be still and hear
The closeness of Your footprints near

Fill this day as You do the sky
With the strength to draw nigh
Held in the Grace that faithfully upholds
As the newness of this dawn unfolds

Teach my heart to walk upon
Each stepping stone leading to Your calm
Reminding my heart You turn night to day
And always lead in Your perfect ways…

The law of the Lord is perfect reviving the soul…
Psalm 19:7

September 17
There's relief from each strain
When I rest in Your Name
There's a reprieve from each care
When I bow to You in prayer

There's reassurance in each step
When I remember You too wept
There's Peace that transforms
When I trust through each storm

There's tenderness that awaits
When I pause to give You thanks
There's Strength on which to stand
When I place all in Your Hands

Give thanks to the Lord,
for He is good;
His love endures forever.
Psalm 107:1

Seek the Lord and His strength,
Seek His face continually.
1 Chronicles 16:11

September 18

You spoke and gave the ability to see
All that came from Your Heart to be
You spoke and gave the ability to hear
Whispered Hope of Your being near

You spoke and history truly began
Before the foundation was visible land
You spoke and the pages began to be filled
With Salvation's Story of peace and goodwill

You spoke and there was day and night
For all to breathe and live in Your Light
You spoke and Grace was unhindered there
Within the Son You did not spare

You spoke and made the only Way
To bring unending change each day
You spoke and there was Hope forevermore
Through unending forgiveness that heals and restores

Praise the Lord, O my soul, and forget not all His benefits
who forgives
all your sins and heals all your diseases,
who redeems your life from the pit
and crowns you with love and compassion,
who satisfies your desires
with good things so that your youth is renewed like the eagle's.
Psalm 103:2-5

September 19

Rest is a gift You alone supply
Neath the covering of Your night sky
Rest is a refueling a needed pace
Neath the wings of Your unending Grace

Rest is a Sabbath of stilled feet
Neath the Cross where forgiveness completes
Rest is a yielding solely unto
Neath the Refuge found in You

Rest is a solace of quiet dreams
Neath the sunrise before it sings
Rest is a posture given to take
Neath the Breath that will never forsake

Rest is a tempo given endlessly
Neath the shadow of Calvary
Rest is a comfort given each day
Neath the Sheltering of You, Yahweh

In repentance and rest is your salvation,
in quietness and trust is your strength.
Isaiah 30:15

September 20

You are the Comforter that brings calm
Through every need that seems beyond
You are the Peace that continually prevails
Through every need without fail

You are the Shepherd that endlessly provides
Through every need felt deep inside
You are the Breath of Hope and renewal
Through every need without refusal

You are the Weaver that wholly completes
Through every need when eyes see defeat
You are the Truth that wholly ignites
Through every need to trust in Your Might

You are the Heart and Hand that extends
Through every need You died to mend
You are the Grace supplying each step
Through every need new mercies are met

*Let us then approach God's throne of grace with confidence,
so that we may receive mercy and find grace
to help us in our time of need.
Hebrews 4:16*

I need Thee
O I need Thee
Every hour I need Thee…
-Robert Lowry, 1872

September 21

The heavens declare the glory of God;
the skies proclaim the work of His Hands.
Day after day they pour forth speech;
night after night they reveal knowledge.
They have no speech, they use no words;
no sound is heard from them.
Psalm 19:1-3

The heavens stunningly declare
That wonders that You placed there
The beauty to daily see
The faithful witness unendingly

The heavens heartily declare
The wonders that are everywhere
The new mercies given each day
The faithfulness of Your gracious ways

The heavens continually declare
The wonders of Your loving care
The abundance You alone designed
The faithfulness within and beyond time

The heavens declare
The wonders You alone prepared
The more than hearts can grasp or imagine
The faithfulness beyond what hearts can fathom

You care for the land and water it. You enrich it abundantly.
The streams of God are filled with water to provide
the people with grain, for so You have ordained it.
Psalm 65:9

September 22
Let night be a reminder the stars still shine
Let day be a reminder You govern time
Let Rest be a reminder You assigned
Let Peace be a reminder You designed

Let breath be a reminder You provide
Let steps be a reminder You supply
Let strength be a reminder You uphold
Let longings be a reminder You enfold

Let Joy be the reminder You instill
Let Promises be the reminder You fulfill
Let Hope be the reminder You impart
Let Grace be the reminder of Your Heart

*But the Advocate, the Holy Spirit,
whom the Father will send in My Name,
will teach you all things and will remind you
of everything I have said to you.
John 14:26*

September 23
*Praise be to the Lord, to God our Savior,
who DAILY bears our burdens.
Psalm 68:19*

Daily intimately faithfully there
Waiting to remove each burden through prayer
Daily intimately faithfully aware
Waiting to replace each burden with care

Daily intimately mercifully here
Waiting patiently for all to draw near
Daily intimately mercifully timed
Waiting patiently for each heart soul and mind…

Daily intimately closer than breath
Waiting patiently for every next step
Daily intimately closer than marrow
Waiting patiently to mend heart sorrow

Daily intimately graciously alive
Waiting patiently Salvation to provide
Daily intimately graciously prepared
Waiting patiently is the Heart that hung there…

*The Lord is not slow in keeping His promise,
as some understand slowness.
Instead He is patient with you,
not wanting anyone to perish,
but everyone to come to repentance.
2 Peter 3:9*

September 24

Tell Him your sorrow tell Him your fears
Tell Him you need to feel Him so near
Tell Him each moment you feel alone
Hear Him tell you that you are His very own

Bring Him decisions that need to be made
Bring Him each hurt in all of your pain
Bring Him your tears in what has been done
Hear Him tell you He bottles each one

Bring Him your heart that's breaking today
Bring Him your mistakes He died to take each away
Bring Him your tiredness He alone will sustain
Hear Him tell you He is Hope that remains

Forget the former things; do not dwell on the past.
See, I am doing a new thing!
I, even I, am He Who blots out your transgressions,
for My own sake, and remember your sins no more.
Isaiah 43:18-19, 25

I must tell Jesus all of my trials,
I cannot bear these burdens alone
In my distress He kindly will help me,
He ever loves and cares for His own.
-Elisha Hoffman, 1894

September 25

Resting alone in Your Covenant care
Trusting alone in Your Grace already there
Leaning alone upon Your Strength each breath
Relying alone for You know what's next

Even while…darkness surrounds
Even until…the trumpet sounds
Even during…unwanted terrain
Even without…desired change

Even though…You are with me
Even if…You are comforting
Even though…You are holding my hand
Even if…You are teaching me to stand

Even though…You are there
Even if…You are aware
Even though…You make a way
Even if…You are Yahweh

*Even though I walk through the valley of the shadow of death,
I will fear no evil, for You are with me…
Psalm 23:4*

*Even if…You are my Sovereign Strength.
Habakkuk 3:17, 19*

September 26
Your consistency and constancy
Unendingly amazes me
Your faithfulness relentlessly
Is wondrously beyond degree

Your graciousness and righteousness
Devotedly is never rushed
Your timeliness and purposefulness
Continuously deepens trust

Your Holiness steadfastly
Renews and restores tirelessly
Your ferventness and peacefulness
Is endlessness of hopefulness

*He wakens me morning by morning,
wakens my ear to listen like one being taught.
Isaiah 50:4*

My hope is built on nothing less,
than Jesus blood and righteousness…
…I rest on His unchanging Grace
-Edward Mote, 1834

September 27

Thank You that Your Peace is greater than the pain
Thank You for Your Strength given that sustains
Thank You that Your Promise is greater than the rain
Thank You for Your Spirit given that remains

Thank You that Your Hope is ever greater than
Thank You for Your Mercy given as Your plan
Thank You that Your Grace is greater than all sin
Thank You for Your Pardon given as Your Amen

Thank You that Your Patience is more prevalent than strain
Thank You for Your Kindness given to obtain
Thank You that Your Comfort is greater than all need
Thank You for Your Joy given to receive

*The Lord will surely comfort Zion
and will look with compassion on all her ruins;
He will make her deserts like Eden, her wastelands
like the garden of the Lord. Joy and gladness will be found in her,
thanksgiving and the sound of singing.
Isaiah 51:3*

September 28

Not in circumstances nor in pain
Is the identity of my name
But in the fact of forgiveness made
To be on earth to sing and proclaim

Jesus Christ my Savior that leads
Through each care and earnest need
Knowing the outcome as night turns to day
Giving renewed Hope to walk in His way

And then my eyes begin to see
Faithfulness beyond my need
The greatest gift of having Him
Is the greatest need deep within

*"For My thoughts are not your thoughts,
neither are your ways My ways," declares the Lord.
"As the heavens are higher than the earth, so are My ways
higher than your ways and My thoughts than your thoughts."
Isaiah 55:8-9*

All the way my Savior leads me,
What have I to ask beside
Can I doubt His tender mercy,
Who through life has been my guide
Heavenly peace divinest comfort,
Here by faith in Him to dwell…
-Fanny Crosby, 1874

September 29

Let this rest on you
I prepared a table to renew
Given to come within this day
Reviving your soul in My perfect way

Let this rest on you
I am the God Who pursues
Reconciling hearts as Mine
Through needed Grace immeasurably divine

Let this rest on you
I am the God Who rescues
Redeeming as the One Who sees
In your midst wholeheartedly

You prepare a table before…me.
Psalm 23:5

The New 23rd by Ralph Carmichael, 1980

September 30
You give Life fuller than the moon
Brighter than any passing gloom
You give Parameters to go or stay
Just like the sunshine precise without delay

You give Guidance to each generation
Just like Eden's first conversation
You give Wisdom for hearts to know
Just like each seed implanted to grow

You give the Fruit that shows Your way
Love Joy and Peace given each day
You give Patient direction and calm
Within Your Kindness to carry on

You give Goodness as the daily scene
Through such Faithfulness like evergreens
You give Gentleness as Your gardening embrace
Through Your selfless forgiving Grace

Let them fear You [with awe-inspired reverence and worship You with obedience] while the sun endures, and as long as the moon [reflects light] throughout all generations.
Psalm 72:5 AMP

Jane Spears

OCTOBER

October 1

Come unto Me,
all who are weary and burdened,
and I will give you rest.
Matthew 11:28

Thank You for teaching my heart to see
You are with me infinitely
There is no end to height nor depth
Within Your promise for every step

Thank You for letting my heart know
The message of Truth infused in my soul
Nothing can separate or stand between
Grace that You give that wholly redeems

Thank You for allowing my heart to hear
Whispers of Hope of Yours ever near
Encircled within Your unending embrace
Until the beginning of the end of this race…

My flesh and my heart may fail, but God is the
strength of my heart and my portion forever.
But as for me, it is good to be near God. I have made the
Sovereign Lord my Refuge; I will tell of all Your deeds.
Psalm 73:26, 28

October 2

You spoke and brought about seasonal change
    You spoke and appointed when to rain
    You spoke and then winds grew calm
    You spoke and chaos turned into song

    You spoke and majestic skies appeared
    You spoke and brought new life right here
    You spoke and starry hosts filled the night
    You spoke and lit each dawn with light

    You spoke and created Love portrayed
    You spoke and promised Hope each day
    You spoke and gave Mercy replacing fear
    You spoke and delivered Grace heart-near

This day is Yours, and Yours also the night;
You established the sun and moon. It was
You who set all the boundaries of the earth;
You made both summer and winter.
Psalm 74:16-17

October 3
Process out loud in grateful praise
Rejoicing in Him for His perfect ways
Give thanks because He is ever near
Leaving no room for doubt or fear

Let the morning quiet overhead
Remind my feet they are Shepherd led
Let the breathtaking stillness become
Thankfulness for the miracle of each one

Let the clouds temporarily placed
Be a reminder of beauty love traced
Let the breaking of this new dawn
Be the springboard of my upraised song

Process out loud through Peace He gives
Rejoicing in His provision to live
Give thanks because He will never forsake
Leaving only room to celebrate

We give thanks to You, O God,
we give thanks, for Your Name is near.
Psalm 75:1

October 4
More You give more to see
More to live through victory
More You speak clearing the way
More within each word You say

Peace You give abundantly
Peace You bring unendingly
Peace Your gift that calms and stills
Peace Your gift that soothes and heals

Grace You give through Your Son
Grace You extend for each to come
Grace Your rhythm of steadfastness
Grace Your Truth of faithfulness

More Peace than can be described
More Grace therein to abide
More Peace that surpasses understanding
More Grace unfathomably heart-landing

*May Grace and Peace be multiplied to you
in the knowledge of God and of Jesus our Lord.
2 Peter 1:2*

October 5
You keep vigil on darkest night
Burning ever Your inextinguishable light
You keep order designed and portrayed
Miraculously through Your Light always

You keep hearts held in place
Through the tempo of Your Grace
You keep showing Your miraculous ways
Ever-Present Help to know each day

You keep governing also the wind
Knowing the moment pain will end
You keep piloting miraculously through
Into the safe harbor defined as You

You will keep in perfect peace
those whose minds are steadfast,
because they trust in You.
Isaiah 26:3

October 6
Desiring a tree that He commanded against
Led to removal from the Garden scent
Desiring something other than Him
Led down the road of destruction within

Desiring fig leaves to hide behind
Led to the first blood shed over mankind
Desiring "wisdom" more than perfection
Led to the chasm between heart and head connection

Desiring Reversal of the decision of ruining
Led to another Garden of pruning
Desiring the debt the first Adam made
Led to the Lamb's blood that saved

Desiring the Mercy that covers more than skin
Led to redemption Grace bought within
Desiring Perfection without end
Led to Jesus forgiving all sin

I have given to them the glory and honor which You have given Me, that they may be one, just as We are one.
John 17:22 AMP

Make Us One by Twila Paris, 2003

October 7
Set your heart on things above
Set your mind on undying love
Set your affection on righteousness
Set your ambition on holiness

Set your heart on Jesus Christ
Set your mind on His sacrifice
Set your affection on Calvary
Set your ambition on humility

Set your Hope on God alone
Set your eyes upon His Throne
Set your listening on hearing His Peace
Set your journeying as resting in His Strength

Let the peace of Christ rule in your hearts…And be thankful.
Let the word of Christ dwell in you richly.
Colossians 3:15, 16

Let him trust in the Name of the Lord, and rely upon his God.
Isaiah 50:10b

October 8
You are our Provisional Care
In our midst You are faithfully there
Walking beside bottling each tear
Calming each heart freeing from fear

You are our Provisional Strength
Immeasurably more than our hearts can think
Holding each close through every change
Through every heartache Your Strength sustains

You are our Provisional Grace
Given sacrificially in our place
More than minds can comprehend
The mercy extended forgiving ALL sin

You are our Provisional Peace
In Your Word that will not cease
You alone are our Life Song
Praising forever to Whom we belong…

The comfort of Your love takes away my fear.
I'll never be lonely, for You are near.
Psalm 23:4b TPT

Little ones to Him belong,
They are weak but He is strong
Yes, Jesus loves me…
-Anna B. Warner, 1860

October 9
You are always righteous, O Lord…
Jeremiah 12:1

You are…Nothing else needed to say
You are…Present in Your unending ways
You are…Wherever I am each day
You are…Whether I am home or far away

You are…And always will be
You are…Greatness beyond degree
You are…More than is meant to comprehend
You are…Ever-before, ever-with always without end

You are among us, O Lord.
Jeremiah 14:9b

I will refresh the weary and satisfy the faint.
Jeremiah 31:25

Way Maker
-Sinach, 2015

October 10
Fret not be still and know
Rest within His sovereign control
Fret not be still and hear
Rest within His words "Do not fear"

Fret not be still and pray
Rest within His answers on the way
Fret not be still and wait
Rest within His timing He correlates

Fret not be still and believe
Rest within His Heart hung on that tree
Fret not be still and find
Rest within His Peace unconfined

Fret not.
Psalm 37:1

The Lord is near.
Philippians 4:5b

And the peace of God, which transcends all understanding,
will guard your hearts and minds in Christ Jesus.
Philippians 4:7

October 11
*Heal me, O Lord, and I will be healed;
save me and I will be saved,
for You are the One I praise.
Jeremiah 17:14*

This is my song in my night
This is my testimony of unending Light
This is my renewed Hope within
This my lifeline deep within

This my prayer become song
This my Truth to stand upon
This my Hope given again
This my Joy without end

You have taught my heart to crave
You Word alone that wholly saves
You have taught my heart to sing
Your Word spoken to revive and cling

ON MY WAY HOME

You have taught my heart to read
Your Word daily to address each need
You have taught my heart to see
Your Word eternal through every scene

You have taught my heart to embrace
Your Word of Life exuding Grace
You have taught my heart each day
Your Word to pray as returned praise

Give thanks to the Lord, for He is good;
His love endures forever.
1 Chronicles 16:34

Heal Me, O Lord
-Jane Spears, 1997

October 12
There becomes yet another granted day
In Your mighty merciful way
Giving kindly another breath to breathe
Displaying Grace wonders for eyes to see

And there You again graciously allow
Another gift to be seen somehow
Upon or among leaves shining through
Heart-shaped kindness formed by You

Intentionally it seems a heart is placed there
To remind my own of Yours once there
To be the Supplier removing all doubt
Of Hope we cannot breathe without

I will praise the Lord no matter what happens.
I will constantly speak of His glories and grace.
I will boast of all His kindness to me.
Let all who are discouraged take heart.
Let us praise the Lord together and exalt His Name.
Psalm 34:1-3 TLB

Holy, Holy, Holy, Lord God Almighty!
Early in the morning our song shall rise to Thee;
Holy, Holy, Holy! Merciful and Mighty!
God in Three Persons, blessed Trinity!
-Reginald Heber, 1826

October 13
Thank You for this gift of time
That Your Heart had in mind
For us to walk together side by side
In the goodness You alone provide

Thank You for the insight to graciously see
The moments You make possible visually
Each picturesque landscape You intentionally made
To revive and sustain through Your Sheltering Shade

Thank You for each quieted faithful step
That You lend to pause and reflect
Upon Your relentless new mercies shown
For gathered hearts to Rest in You alone…

Whoever dwells in the shelter of the Most High
will rest in the shadow of the Almighty.
Psalm 91:1

October 14
No place is without Your intersecting Grace
No moment experienced without Your embrace
No breath without encouragement to breathe through
No instance ever without the Mercy of You

Each place miraculously bears Your Name
Each moment inspires Your Love unchanged
Each breath encourages the next to come
Each instance is filled with Mercy in each one

Each place holds Your Truth meant to know
Each moment provides Your Way to go
Each breath depends upon You to live
Each instance is Mercy filled that You give

May our Lord Jesus Christ Himself and God our Father, who loved us and by His grace gave us eternal encouragement and good hope, encourage your hearts and strengthen you in every good deed and word.
2 Thessalonians 2:16-17

October 15
Beautifully broken buried seed into flower
Graciously spoken Mercy each hour
Willingly broken like the alabaster jar
Permanently scarred for all to come as they are

Beautifully broken for every broken heart
Graciously spoken into the deepest parts
Willingly broken for all to receive
Permanently scarred love extended through Calvary

He was pierced for our transgressions, He was crushed for our iniquities; the punishment that brought us peace was on Him, and by His wounds we are healed.
Isaiah 53:3

Just as I am, Thou wilt receive,
Wilt welcome, pardon, cleanse, relieve.
Because Thy promise I believe,
O Lamb of God, I come, I come!
-Charlotte Elliott, 1836

October 16

"You will seek Me and find Me
when you seek Me with all your heart.
I will be found by you," declares the Lord.
Jeremiah 29:13-14a

What a profound promise You had written down
For Your Heart to be sought then found
You are not a God far away
But closer than breath You give each day

How intimately close Your Heart beats
Nearer than near ever within reach
That knowingly brings change to steps
When Invisible Grace has been met…

Now to the King eternal, immortal, invisible, the only God,
be honor and glory for ever and ever. Amen.
1 Timothy 1:17

The Lord bless you and keep you;
the Lord make His face shine upon you
and be gracious to you;
the Lord turn His face toward you
and give you peace.
Numbers 6:24-26

October 17
Thank You for Your surrender that brought life-giving change
Thank You for being the Heavenly Hope prearranged
Thank You for the sacrifice given that day
Thank You that sins were completely washed away

Thank You for Your Grace our reversal to grief
Thank You for being our lifeline of Peace
Thank You for reflecting Heaven's Heart
Thank You for Your gallery of everlasting art

Thank You for Your outward continual provision
Thank You for Your inward Gift for all Your forgiven
Thank You for Your recorded prayer that You prayed
Thank You for Your desire for all to be saved

Father, I want those You have given
Me to be with Me where I am,
and to see My glory, the glory
You have given Me because You loved Me
before the creation of the world.
Righteous Father, though the world
does not know You, I know You,
and they know that You have sent Me.
I have made You known to them,
and will continue to make You known in order
that the love You have for Me
may be in them and that I Myself may be in them.
John 17:24-26

October 18

You are the Strength supplied for each test
As in Samson's final prayer request
You are the Calm in the midst of the storm
As in the Disciples who were weary and worn

You are the Light given as planned
As in the first day when the world began
You are the Source multiplying each seed
As in the meeting of Joseph's immeasurable need

You are the Radiance shining through each sorrowful woe
As in the direction of Jonathan's bow and arrows
You are the Giver of each mission to complete
As in Jonah's surprise ride redirecting his feet

You are the Truth given miraculously to each ear
As in forgiveness to know and draw near
You are the Redemption providing heart change
As in the Book of Life of each written name

For where your treasure is, there your heart will be also.
Luke 12:34

October 19
Your faithfulness and consistency
Are set in the heavens for all to see
Daily new wonders and mercies are placed
By your Hand of compassionate Grace

Your order promised provided and proclaimed
Are set in the heavens that bear Your Name
No tongue on earth can truly describe
Your faithfulness permitted profoundly prescribed

Your faithfulness is meant to be experienced
Within Your laws of nature You created nearness
Provided through Jesus Christ as Emmanuel
Opening the heavens through the torn veil…

One more day to sing alleu
One more day granted by You
One more day for Your purpose driven
One more day faithfully given

One more day the morning to greet
One more day to lay all at Your feet
One more day to walk within
One more day as newness begins

One more day faithfulness to know
One more day graciously bestowed
One more day in between
One last day alleu's dream

*I will declare that Your love stands firm forever,
that You have established Your faithfulness in heaven itself.
The heavens praise Your wonders, Lord, Your faithfulness too,
in the assembly of the holy ones.
Who is like You, Lord God Almighty?
You, Lord, are mighty, and Your faithfulness surrounds You.
Psalm 89:2, 5, 8*

Praise God from Whom all blessings flow;
Praise Him all creatures here below;
Praise Him above ye heavenly hosts;
Praise Father, Son, and Holy Ghost.
Amen.
-Thomas Ken, 1674

October 20
Peace His overarching guarding Grace
Peace His Might through whatever is faced
Peace His spoken word heard within
Peace His strength given without end

Peace His gift of undisturbed calm
Peace His promise to rest upon
Peace His provision endlessly supplied
Peace His faithfulness relentlessly abides

And the peace of God, which transcends all powers of thought, will be a garrison to guard your hearts and minds in Christ Jesus.
Philippians 4:7 (Weymouth)

The wilderness and the solitary place shall be glad for them; and the desert shall rejoice; and blossom as the rose.
Isaiah 35:1

October 21
You spoke the exact words I needed to hear
To not let resentment take over or interfere
To trust in what has temporarily come
That good is sovereignly Your outcome

Grow my trust in Your perfect ways
Teach my footsteps of temporary clay
To rest in your sovereignty all of my days
No matter the circumstances that temporarily may stay

Thank You that You came to restore
The vessels You created to live as never before
To experience such Mercy and endless Grace
With You beside guiding the pace…

Let us hold unswervingly to the hope we profess,
for He who promised is faithful.
Hebrews 10:23

Step By Step
-Rich Mullins, 1991

October 22

Teach us to number our days aright,
that we may gain a heart of wisdom.
Psalm 90:12

You are our daily Treasure to find
In the footprints You left behind
Directing our steps to follow Your lead
Trusting each step is a gift received

You reassure Your Presence each day
In Your Word that says "walk this way"
Hearing You speak is the treasured lifeline
And sweetest communion set within time

Your ears shall hear a word behind you, saying,
"This is the way, walk in it."
Isaiah 30:12

I hear the Savior say
"Thy strength indeed is small
Child of weakness, watch and pray
Find in Me thine all in all."
-Elvina M. Hall, 1865

October 23
You know how I need reminding every day
That You are with me now and always
You know how many times I tend to forget
That You are forever my unending Gift

You know how my thoughts need to recall
That You are faithful and Lord over all
You know how often my lungs need to breathe
That You are Greatness that nothing against can succeed

You know how long the journey will be
That You walk beside attentively
You know how much I need to hear
That You are whispering there's no need to fear

There hath not failed one word of all His promises.
1 Kings 8:56

October 24
The Lord is my Shepherd,
I shall not want.
He makes me lie down in green pastures,
He leads me beside still waters,
He restores my soul.
He guides me in paths of righteousness for His Name's sake.
Psalm 23:1-3

Find Rest within the Shepherd's care
His God-breathed promise is faithfully there
Being the Answer for our greatest need
His gift of gracious unending Peace

Find Strength within His pastures green
Listening to His God-breathed dream
Of full dependence upon His Shepherding
That gives each voice His breath to sing

Cares Chorus
-Kelly Willard, 1978

Burdens Are Lifted At Calvary
-John M. Moore, 1952

October 25
Worn out binding held day by day
Your Word inviting given to say
Come hear listen and grow
In My Grace that overflows

Yes I left My Word for you
To find My Hope perpetually infused
Inside the depths of where you would be
Was my plan on Calvary

And as you see each dawn appear
You breathe in reassurance that I am near
No other place have I chosen to provide
Than your heart for My Peace to reside

You have made known to me the path of life;
You will fill me with joy in Your Presence.
Acts 2:28

October 26
King Of My Heart, 2015

Awoke hearing this enfolding tune
Laying there letting it fill the room
Basking in the message therein
That Good is Who You are without end

Thank You for letting my heart hear
This beautiful message softly near
Reminding me once again my whole must
Is to dwell within the heart space of trust

Where You lead You fully understand
How much I need the goodness of Your Hand
Where by faith each step is placed
And that each one is met with Good Grace

Into each season implanted there
Is Grace sufficient for EVERY care
Just like a Monarch guided on his way
Finds Your faithfulness awaiting each day

For You, Lord, are the Most High over all the earth;
You are exalted far above all gods.
Psalm 97:9

October 27
Thank You for Your provisional Grace
That impacts this daily footrace
Thank You for Your provisional Strength
That brings individualized heart relief

Thank You for Your provisional equipping
Through puzzling moments You are never missing
Thank You for Your provisional attentiveness
Administering Hope found only in Jesus

Thank You for Your provisional Scars
Healing eternally each one of ours
Thank You for Your provisional Peace
The theme of Rest found at Your Feet

Behold what provisional manner indeed
That we alone by Grace are freed
Behold what provisional manner to believe
That Jesus died for you and me…

Behold, God is my Helper and Ally; The Lord is the Sustainer of my soul [my upholder].
Psalm 54:4 AMP

Behold What Manner Of Love
-Patricia Lynn Van, 1978

October 28
Grace and Peace be yours in abundance through
the knowledge of God and of Jesus our Lord.
2 Peter 1:2

Grace and Peace abundant as autumn rain
Falling upon all to bring promised change
To the very ground the Gardener prepared
For every heart to find His there

Grace and Peace abundantly flows
For every heart His love to know
Within the bounds of time and gardening space
His Heart of forgiveness implanted through Grace

Grace and Peace abundantly come
Wrapped as a Gift to everyone
No longer in a manger or bed of hay
But on Heaven's Throne since His Resurrection Day

Grace and Peace abundant as autumn rain
Given to bring eternal change
Through the forgiveness available each day
Given through the abundant Grace of Yahweh

On My Way Home

But because of His great love for us, God, who is rich in mercy, made us alive with Christ even when we were dead in transgressions—it is by grace you have been saved. And God raised us up with Christ and seated us with Him in the heavenly realms in Christ Jesus.
Ephesians 2:4-6

Peace, peace, wonderful peace,
Coming down from the Father above!
Sweep over my spirit forever, I pray,
In fathomless billows of love!
-Warren D. Cornell, 1889

October 29

*For we are God's workmanship,
created in Christ Jesus to do good works,
which God prepared in advance for us to do.
Ephesians 2:10*

Let me walk in the path You have prepared
Let me be found listening to You there
Let me grow deeper in depths throughout time
Let me lean solely upon You as the Vine

Let me find rest considering outcomes ahead
Let me remember each step is Shepherd led
Let me be found relying upon Your Might
Let me live surrendered both day and night

I surrender all, I surrender all
All to Thee my Blessed Savior, I surrender all
-Judson W. Van De Venter, 1896

October 30
You are and were and remain
The Word forever spoken unchanged
Steadfast Heart that sustains
Before yet with forever the same

The finite cannot comprehend
Immeasurable Grace given without end
Founder and Fountain giving inside
Salvation that only You willingly provide

Freely given freely to restore
The stolen innocence taken on as never before
The priceless Gift no debtor could pay
Decided upon before there was a first day

Amazing Grace amazing provision
From Heaven's Heart to be pardon's decision
Amazing Mercy that came to endure
The only Way to make sinners pure

But You remain the same, and Your years will never end.
Hebrews 1:12, Psalm 102:27

Amazing Grace how sweet the sound…
-John Newton, 1779

October 31
You gave the tempo and echoing pace
Guiding to Sinai's fireplace
You gave the fulfillment timed and placed
Guiding to Gethsemane's Garden of Grace

You gave unendingly multiplied Bread
Guiding through each desert manna led
You gave astonishment to shepherds by night
Guiding to Bethlehem's inextinguishable Light

You gave Testimony without end
Guiding as the Alpha and Amen
You gave once for all to wholly embrace
Guiding to Heaven's sanctuary of Grace

In Your unfailing love
You will lead the people You have redeemed.
In Your Strength You will guide them to Your holy dwelling.
Exodus 15:13

He leadeth me, He leadeth me,
By His own Hand He leadeth me.
-J. H. Gilmore, 1862

NOVEMBER

November 1
Your Word continually brings a smile to my face
To read and find rest as Your gracious pace
No other place extended to be
A river of calm directed inwardly

Your Word continually brings the choice
To quietly listen to Your voice
Then be reminded of how time blends
Hope through Grace that does not end

Your Word continually reveals each day
Unending Mercy extended to clay
Timeless You are yet written within
Each heart page to find where Grace begins

Let us then approach God's throne of grace with confidence, so that we may receive mercy and find grace to help us in our time of need.
Hebrews 4:16

Thy Word is a lamp unto my feet and a light unto my path.
Psalm 119:105

November 2
Nothing to bring
But surrendering
Nothing to say
But to pray

Nothing to see
But believe
Nothing to hear
But do not fear

Nothing to own
But Grace alone
Noting to decide
But to abide

The Lord is my Shepherd,
I lack nothing…
Psalm 23:1

Whom have I in heaven but You?
And earth has nothing I desire besides You.
Psalm 73:25

November 3
You meet each need met in each day
You hold each hand without delay
You know the outcome before the test
You give ahead the prayer of rest

You bring peace and still the soul
You speak and calm each step to go
You breathe and anchor Hope within
You teach and console once again

You instruct and counsel more yet to be known
You light and reflect the way to be shown
You lead and guide through valleys and hills
You shepherd and supply the waters stilled…

*I will instruct you and teach you in the way you should go;
I will counsel you with My loving eye on you.
Psalm 32:8*

*He leads me beside quiet waters…
Psalm 23:2b*

November 4
There an opening of quiet dawn
There renewed strength to lean upon
There visible beauty once again
There repeated faithfulness to rest within

There quiet moments fade into day
There renewed mercies straight from Yahweh
There guided steps intentionally
There each one timed perfectly

There quietness brings the gift of calm
There tenderness provided to encamp upon
There spoken beauty filling the skies
There whispered Peace of His Heart nearby…

The Lord gives Strength to His people;
the Lord blesses His people with Peace.
Psalm 29:11

When peace like a river attendeth my way…
. Thou hast taught me to say,
"It is well, it is well with my soul'
-Horatio Spafford, 1873

November 5
May the need become a benefit
That hearts cannot possibly forget
May the portion become an extreme
That hearts cannot possibly miss the means

May the footprints become the way
That hearts cannot possibly be led astray
May the yielding become the choice
That hearts cannot possibly follow another voice

May the thoughts become softened clay
That hearts cannot possibly refute to obey
May the wrestling become replaced with peace
That hearts cannot possibly disbelieve

May the pursuit become pliable surrender
That hearts cannot possibly fail to remember
May the wandering become the summit's view
That hearts cannot possibly miss being made new

Create in me a clean heart, O God,
and renew a steadfast spirit within me.
Psalm 51:10

November 6
Noah Daniel and Job held a common thread
Hopeless circumstance through each were led
Of impossible survival against all odds
If not alone for the Grace of God

Held what a beautiful place
Held by embodied Grace
Held by assurance no matter what
Held by Love that never stops

Held within nail-pierced Hands
Held within Mercy's plan
Held within when weary and tried
Held within Strength to abide

Held through moments of silent nights
Held through moments of seeking insight
Held through moments of required waiting
Held through moments of entrusted initiating

Held by faithfulness
Held within guardedness
Held through embodied Grace
Held what a most beautiful place

So do not fear, for I am with you;
do not be dismayed, for I am your God.
I will strengthen you and help you;
I will uphold you with My righteous right hand.
Isaiah 41:10

November 7
Thank You for the morning's embrace
Felt like the wind upon my face
Delivering change a patterned placed
Set in motion by Your Grace

The birds created to sing and soar
Heard by ears to pause and adore
The Giver of each noted sound
Authoring Peace eternally inbound

So let my heart trustingly be
Driven by Your breath steadfastly
Sometimes felt ofttimes seen
Individual moments encased as Your dreams

The Spirit of God has made me;
the breath of the Almighty gives me life.
Job 33:4

November 8
Thank You for Peace that remains
As a constant through every change
Thank You for Tenderness You provide
For every heartache carried inside

Thank You for Mercy that covers each part
Within the chambers of broken hearts
Thank You for Hope You planned in advance
To hold onto in every circumstance

Thank You for Comfort within the storm
Holding fast each heart that mourns
Thank You for Constancy in uncharted waters
Where You tirelessly sustain each son and daughter

Thank You for Goodness that will never stop
Through calendar moments each Grace-bought
Thank You for Prayer given to pray
Thy Will be done…have Thine own way…

How priceless is Your unfailing love, O God! People take refuge in the shadow of Your wings.
Psalm 36:7

Thou art the Potter, I am the clay…
-Adelaide A. Pollard, 1906

November 9
You take my feelings and neediness
And wrap them in Your robe of righteousness

You take my heartache and brokenness
And wrap them gingerly in Your Holiness

You take the sin that I cannot bear
And wrapped them in thorns You chose to wear

You take away the tears You knew I would cry
And wrapped them in remembrance as You chose to die

You take away my heart dilemma in unanswered prayer
And wrap them in Your timing and wait with me there…

*They that dwell under His shadow shall return;
they shall revive as the corn, and grow as the vine.
Hosea 14:7 AKJV*

November 10
Guide the pace and each rest stop
Teaching nothing is for not
Guide the steps where You lead
Teaching impossible through Yours is achieved

Guide the inertia to onward go
Teaching Your timing is never slowed
Guide the path with forked roads
Teaching clarity lifts the load

Guide the mind on the trail
Teaching difficulties do not prevail
Guide the heart to continually hear
Teaching Yours is endlessly near

*When you pass through the waters, I will be with you;
and through the rivers, they shall not overflow you.
Isaiah 43:2*

Guide me, O Thou Great Jehovah,
Pilgrim through this barren land;
I am weak, but Thou art mighty;
Hold me with Thy powerful hand.
-William Williams, 1745

November 11
A Veteran's Prayer

There's not a day without You
Hold me steadfast beyond war's view
There's not a day without light
Help me remember this through the night

There's not a moment that You didn't see
Help me in the aftermath inwardly
There's not a moment You don't know
Help me remember You love me so

There's not a place You cannot be
Help me remember Your Sovereignty
There's not a place You cannot provide
Hold me steadfast with Your Peace inside

*Blessed are those who have learned to acclaim You,
who walk in the light of Your Presence, O Lord.
Psalm 89:15*

In honor of each answered prayer
that carried each Veteran's heart home…

November 12
You are in the midst everywhere
But exact and precise in being there
Placed among and deep within
Leading yet strengthening without end

You are the answer in the midst
Bringing peace to all the what ifs
Placed within hearts to rest
In Your Word of faithfulness

You are the assurance that exists
Speaking calm in the midst
Reminding hearts to hold onto
The steadfast Hope found in You

*Now faith is confidence in what we hope for
and assurance about what we do not see.
Hebrews 11:1*

My faith looks up to Thee
Thou Lamb of Calvary, Savior Divine!
-Ray Palmer, 1830

November 13
You remind me of how close You truly are
Underneath Your created stars
Ever-Present every day
Ever close in beautiful ways

You remind me that the clouds that come
Never hide me from Your Son
Ever-Present every day
Ever beside in beautiful ways

You remind me that Your Spirit enfolds
Shepherding me to truly know
You are Ever- Present every day
Ever inside in beautiful ways

Escort me into Your Truth;
take me by the hand and teach me.
For You are the God of my salvation;
I have wrapped my heart into Yours all day long!
Psalm 25:5 TPT

Great are the works of the Lord, they are pondered by all who delight in them.
Glorious and majestic are His deeds, and His righteousness endures forever.
He has caused His wonders to be remembered; the Lord is gracious and compassionate.
Psalm 111:2-4

November 14
There given a belt to see
In the night sky specifically
To shine exact and spatially be
Changeless measurement perfectly

Today a given belt to wear
Fitted through the gift of prayer
To shine the Truth that sets hearts free
Through measureless Grace specifically

He who made the Pleiades and Orion,
who turns midnight into dawn and darkens day into night,
who calls for the waters of the sea and pours them
out over the face of the land the Lord is His Name.
Amos 5:8

Even in darkness light dawns…
Psalm 112:4

November 15
Thank You that You know the complete story
And every detail used for Your Glory
Thank You that there are no missing parts
That are not known by Your Heart

Thank You that You walk each through
To behold Your miracles on the move
Thank You for each step of faith
Completely known that You celebrate

Thank You for each part You wrote
For Your Bride to know Your vote
Thank You that Your love is fierce
And that it is known by Your side that was pierced

Thank You for Your Story of Grace
That holds each heart through allotted faith
Thank You that Your holy supply
Holds us each as the apple of Your eye

Keep me as the apple of Your eye;
hide me in the shadow of Your wings.
Psalm 17:8

November 16
Thank You for still giving a song to sing
About the joy that You alone bring
Instilling exact words into a heart
To be sung with the breath Yours imparts

Thank You for still calming the sea
In the deepest depths faithfully
Where You still walk holding each hand
Through Unseen footprints as You planned

Thank You for still speaking always
Through Your Word as strength for each day
Bethlehem's Bread to gather and embrace
Gethsemane's answer as personalized Grace

It is good for our hearts to be strengthened by Grace
Hebrews 13:8b

The joy of the Lord is my strength.
Nehemiah 8:10

Yet I am always with You; You hold me by my right hand.
You guide me with Your counsel, and afterward You will take me
into glory.
Psalm 73:23-24

November 17

Oh the Rest of being still
Oh the Grace in surrendered will
Oh the Mercy undeserved
Oh the Holy Spirit unreserved

Oh the Light exposing awe
Oh the Restoration laid on straw
Oh the Gift above all things
Oh the Hallelujah the forgiven sing

You are my Only Place of Rest
You are my Only Peace through each test
You are my Only Provision that sustains
You are my Only Strength that remains

You are my Only Comfort in every breath
You are my Only Solace in every step
You are my Only Guide directing the pace
You are my Only Hope of unfathomable Grace

*...because of the surpassing measure of God's grace
[His undeserved favor, mercy, and blessing which is revealed]
in you. Now thanks be to God for His indescribable gift
[which is precious beyond words]!
2 Corinthians 9:14-15 AMP*

Come every soul by sin oppressed
there's mercy with the Lord
and He will surely give you rest
by trusting in His Word
Only trust Him...
-John Stockton, 1874

November 18
Thank You for the calm You alone bring
In the gift of surrendering
Thank You for the words given to sing
In the gift of following

Thank You for the rhythm of Your pace
In the gift of steadfast Grace
Thank you for the guidance knowingly ahead
In the gift of being Shepherd led

Thank You for the timing of answered prayer
In the gift of burdens shared
Thank You for the momentary to walk through
In the gift of knowing You

Therefore we do not lose heart.
Though outwardly we are wasting away,
yet inwardly we are being renewed day by day.
For our light and momentary troubles are achieving for us an
eternal glory that far outweighs them all.
2 Corinthians 2:16-17

For great is His love toward us,
and the faithfulness of the Lord endures forever.
Praise the Lord.
Psalm 117:2

November 19
Thou shalt quicken me again…
Psalm 71:10 KJV

Quicken revive and restore
This is the work You do Lord
Changing the lifeless enabling response
Through unfailing love Your Heart has launched

Quicken revive and restore
Today again as You have before
Allowing the gift of breath you share
To be returned in praise and prayer

Quicken revive and restore
Your Heart plan forevermore
For all to see the work already done
Through Jesus Christ as Your Kingdom come

The Lord is my Strength and my Song;
He has become my Salvation.
Psalm 118:14

November 20
He gives us more Grace than we can comprehend
As Savior Redeemer yet closest Friend
He gives us more Mercy new every day
As Creator Sustainer that washes sin away

He gives us more Blessings each day to behold
As Giver of even a caterpillar on the road
He gives us more Strength as Autumn leaves
As Hope will remind after Winter is Spring

He gives us more Kindness than can be imagined
As Surrendered beyond no heart can fathom
He gives us more Peace than a lifetime can define
As Messiah King yet Shepherd called mine…

*For it is by grace you have been saved, through
faith and this is not from yourselves it is the gift of God…
Ephesians 2:8*

Blessed Jesus, blessed Jesus
Thou has bought us, Thine we are…
-Savior Like A Shepherd Lead Us, 1836

November 21
Walk beside her once again
Through this trial bring an end
That will amaze and glorify
How You answered before our eyes

Walk beside her in every step
Let her feel Your very breath
In ways that comfort by design
In mercy wonders given on time

Walk beside her carry her through
Moments fully known each by You
Let her experience knowingly
Peace encompassing tenderly

Walk beside her holding her hand
Infusing Hope as Your plan
Relaying daily as knees bend
Enfolding Grace without end

The Lord is full of compassion and mercy.
James 5:11b

November 22
Thank You for the way You lead
Shepherding where You intercede
Guiding with Your rhythmic pace
Where Your staff is loving Grace

Thank You for such tenderness
That You chose to render us
With Your whispers near enough
To experience Your forgiving touch

Thank You for restful Peace
In the stillness providing strength
Restoring the weary to live renewed
Through quieted moments alone with You

The Lord is my Shepherd;
I have all that I need.
He lets me rest in green meadows;
He leads me beside peaceful streams.
He renews my strength.
He guides me along right paths,
bringing honor to His Name.
Psalm 23:1-3 NLT

November 23
Prepare ye the way of the Lord.
Isaiah 40:3

You are the prepared Grace of our thanksgiving
You are the prepared Goodness among the living
You are the prepared Hope that is Heart driven
You are the prepared Blessing that is life-giving

You are our prepared Portion…selflessly
You are our prepared Provision…unfailingly
You are our prepared Purpose…knowingly
You are our prepared Peace…faithfully

Come Thou Fount of every blessing...
-Robert Robinson, 1758

November 24
Thank You for where You speak
Thank You for what You teach
Thank You for how You know
Thank You for there You flow

The Lord is there.
Ezekiel 48:35

By His wounds you have been healed
By His Grace mercy revealed
By His wisdom surpassing Peace
By His Might unending Strength

By His Word infallible
By His touch unfathomable
By His promise immutable
By His Presence unshakeable

The earth is filled with Your love, O Lord;
teach me Your decrees.
Psalm 119:64

For You have given me hope.
Psalm 119:49

November 25

Now to Him who is able to do exceedingly abundantly above all that we ask or think, according to the power that works in us.
Ephesians 3:20 NKJV

God is able beyond
Exceedingly abundantly every new dawn
Above all yet continually within
Giving His power that has no end

God is able no matter what
Exceedingly abundantly at every road stop
Above the worries beyond each care
Giving His answers powerfully shared

God is able before and behind
Exceedingly abundantly graced moments designed
Above all else His Heart to find
Giving His power to become like-mind…

ON MY WAY HOME

May the wonder continuously be
The Grace found hung upon that Tree
May the beauty eyes continuously see
The miracle of Redemption perfectly

May the song continuously become
The surrender of hearts ransomed as one
May the words continuously form
The gratitude of worship that adores

O come let us adore Him…
-John Francis Wade, 1744

November 26

*Shadrach, Meshach and Abednego replied to him,
"King Nebuchadnezzar, we do not need to
defend ourselves before you in this matter.
If we are thrown into the blazing furnace, the God
we serve is able to deliver us from it,
and He will deliver us from your Majesty's hand.
But even if He does not, we want you to know, your Majesty, that
we will not serve your gods or worship
the image of gold you have set up."
Daniel 3:16-18*

Three surrendered hearts completely sold out
Stood their ground without a doubt
No way were they going to bow down
To the gold idol at the music's sound

Even if…they were thrown into a furnace
Even if…they stated "nothing would turn us"
Even if…they would not turn away
Even if…they would only serve the God Who saves

The chance was given the music began
The knees did not bow from any of them
The soldiers bound the three without debate
And threw them into the fire to incinerate

But immediately a miracle took place
Unbound in the fire walking by Grace
Though in the fire they burned not
Except for their hearts for God that would not stop

Into the fire though untouched
Protected by God Whom they loved so much
They were unwilling to serve another
Except for the One they knew as no other…

Your Word, Lord, is eternal; it stands firm in the heavens.
Your faithfulness continues through all generations;
You established the earth, and it endures. Your laws endure
to this day, for all things serve You. To all perfection I see a limit,
but Your commands are boundless.
Psalm 119:89-91, 96

Even if…yet I will…
Habakkuk 3:17-18

November 27

O the Hope that shines through the dark
O the Hope You alone impart
O the Hope that filled the skies
O the Hope You alone supplied

O the Hope that became real
O the Hope You alone instill
O the Hope that brings change
O the Hope You alone became

O the Hope that will not cease
O the Hope You alone increase
O the Hope that is never far
O the Hope You alone are

O the Hope that is Grace-willed
O the Hope You alone fulfilled
O the Hope that grants insight
O the Hope You alone ignite

As a light that shines in a dark place, until the day dawns and the morning star rises in your hearts…
2 Peter 1:19

November 28
Faithfulness is a direction that flows
From Your devotion to every soul
Faithfulness is a coverage divine
From Your devotion set in time

Faithfulness is an action that is found
From Your devotion that wholly astounds
Faithfulness is present in the lion's den
From Your devotion rescuing hearts within

Faithfulness is character on display
From Your devotion in countless ways
Faithfulness is consistent precise and exact
From Your devotion with eternal impact

Who is like You, Lord God Almighty? You, Lord, are mighty, and Your faithfulness surrounds You.
Psalm 89:8

Great is Thy Faithfulness,
Great is Thy Faithfulness
Morning by morning…
-Thomas Chisholm, 1923

November 29
Lord, my life is in Your Hands
Led by Grace as You planned
You direct my path to find
Peace supplied to breathe as mine

Lord, every moment every step
Is Shepherded and fully kept
Through morning mercies there by You
Peace supplied that strengthens to renew

Lord, all of time You sovereignly know
Leading through valleys here below
Holding hearts by Yours alone
Peace supplied by Mercy shown

*The Lord will guide you always; He will satisfy your needs
in a sun-scorched land and will strengthen your frame.
Isaiah 58:11*

*My times are in Your Hands.
Psalm 31:15*

November 30
All Your words are true; all Your righteous laws are eternal.
Psalm 119:160

In and through Your Might and Name
There is Rest from You unchanged
In and through unending ways
There is Strength from You always

In and through Your Word that speaks
There is the Gift of unending Peace
In and through Your Heart You gave
There is forgiveness from the empty grave

O how Your Word touches the depths of my soul
The flood of memories when You made me whole
From brokenness to finding Rest within
Reading Your Testament again and again

O how Your Word has become my delight
In the hardest places You have preserved my life
Teaching my heart the Hope You alone bring
Has become the crown of my thanksgiving

Let me live that I may praise You; and may Your laws sustain me.
Psalm 119:175

JANE SPEARS

DECEMBER

December 1

Truth is seen in Him and you, because the darkness is passing and the true light is already shining.
1 John 2:8

Thank You for encircled Grace
Through the arms of Your embrace
Thank You for surrounding Rest
Through Your song lullaby expressed

Thank You for unending Peace
Through the whispered words You speak
Thank You for everlasting Atonement
Through the hard in temporary moments

Thank You for Your encompassing power
Through Your gift of quiet each hour
Thank You for ceaseless eternity
Through the momentum of Your Sovereignty

The Lord is my portion, therefore I will wait for Him.
Lamentations 3:24

Then sings my soul…

December 2

The expanse of amazing can be seen everyday
By unending faithfulness on display
Cloud appointed moments that winds obey
Form hearts and crosses of love that stays

The mirror imaging that water reflects
Exactly what's there and nothing less
Like on a mission of a timeless embrace
Framed as a wonder of permanent Grace

The morning dance in the skies
Unveils beauty before each sunrise
Like a prepared table set in place
To find sweet rest in splashes of Grace

And sometimes beauty has a sound
In peace be still therein newfound
Of drinking in Heaven's rhapsody
His Song unending joyously

It's here in Your Presence, in Your sanctuary, where I learn more of Your ways, for holiness is revealed in everything You do. Lord, You're the One and Only, the great and glorious God!
Your display of wonders, miracles,
and power makes the nations acknowledge You.
Psalm 77:13-14 TPT

He rules the world with truth and grace
and makes the nation prove
the glories of His righteousness
and wonders of His love.
-Isaac Watts, 1719

December 3
*I wait for the Lord, my whole being waits,
and in His Word I put my hope.
Psalm 130:5*

Peace be within you My beloved one
There is quietness as you willingly come
Peace be within you each new dawn
This is My provision to lean upon

Peace be within you no matter the waves
There is nothing too difficult hear what I say
Peace be within you as My unending song
Therein hear My promise lasting your lifelong

Thank You for the Peace You alone give
Strengthening my heart to fully live
Thank You for Your unending ways
That renews my heart through Your Word each day

*I will say, "Peace be within you."
Psalm 122:8*

December 4
Thank You for this time alone
To rest within Your Heart enthroned
So high and lifted up yet near
As if a whisper heard crystal clear

Thank You for the Hope You speak
To rest within as quieted peace
The rhythm found beyond to seek
Beside Your Heart of rested feet

Thank You for being timeless Grace
Where hearts can find their resting place
In Your devotion always giving toward
Entrusted hearts surrendered as Yours

You are my Hope my Peace
You are my Joy my Strength
You are my Savior my Grace
You are my Shepherd my resting place…

I lift up my eyes to You,
to You who sit enthroned in heaven.
Psalm 123:1

December 5
The place made to sing
Neath the shadow of Your wing
The place given to cling
In the midst of everything

The place made to completely know
Where feet can abide that You love so
The place given to wholly hear
Revealed solace unendingly near

The place made to behold
Sheltered care that tenderly enfolds
The place given to graciously see
Attentiveness steadfastly…

Because You are my Help, I sing in the shadow of Your wing.
I cling to You; Your right hand upholds me.
Psalm 63:7-8

O for the wonderful love He has promised
Promised for you and for me
Though we have sinned He has mercy and pardon
Pardon for you and for me
-Will L. Thompson, 1880

December 6
You walk beside in sickness and pain
You walk beside and faithfully remain
You walk beside leading the way
You walk beside guiding each day

You are the Protector over my lungs
Through each breath yet to come
You are the Protector over my heart
Lighting each step through the dark

There is no moment unknown to You
There are only moments of being carried through
There is no moment You do not see
There are only moments of Love unconditionally

You are faithfully with us every step
Through every heartache Your promise is kept
By Your Name Emmanuel Forever with us come to dwell

You are the Name above all names
Yet willingly chose to be the offering of change
The Greatest saving the lowest to impart
Amazing Grace for every heart

...because of the truth, which lives in us and will be with us forever: Grace, mercy and peace from God the Father and from Jesus Christ, the Father's Son, will be with us in truth and love.
2 John 1:2-3

As the mountains surround Jerusalem,
so the Lord surrounds His people both now and forevermore.
Psalm 125:2
(Holy hug...wholly loved...)

December 7

Thankful for Your bed of hay
That held Salvation on Christmas Day
Thankful for Your visitors that came
That held a moment they would not trade

Thankful for Your inextinguishable Light
That held out comfort that holy night
Thankful for Your growing years
That held the tools of drawing near

Thankful for Your selfless ministry
That held the teaching of Your Deity
Thankful for Your Word You spoke
That held the gift of endless Hope

Thankful for Your willingness to die
That held out Mercy crucified
Thankful for Your empty tomb
That held the Grace to fill each room

Thankful for Your Holy Spirit supplied
That held the guidance for Your Bride
Thankful for Your Kingdom come
That held the promise of Your Will be done

On My Way Home

So now wrap your heart tightly around the hope that lives within us, knowing that God always keeps His promises!
Hebrews 10:23 TPT

The Lord has done great things for us, and we are filled with joy.
Psalm 126:3

Away in a manger no crib for a bed
There is a place of quiet rest near to the Heart of God
The little Lord Jesus laid down His sweet head
A place where sin cannot molest near to the Heart of God
The stars in the sky looked down where He lay
O Jesus blessed Redeemer sent from the Heart of God
The little Lord Jesus asleep on the hay
Hold us who wait before Thee near to the Heart of God
-Away in a Manger, Unknown, 1885
-Near to the Heart of God, Cleland McAfee, 1903

December 8
More than letters that form a word
More like an action completely unearned
More from within given to another
More of this fruit that affects like no other

More to become for others to receive
More benefiting giver as well as the need
More like a current that touches not to stay
More in abundance from the Heart of Yahweh

More of this one word throughout time
More in the moments given by design
More of the blessings He had in mind
More of the heartfelt gift of being kind

Kind words are like honey –
sweet to the soul
and healthy for the body.
Proverbs 16:24 NLT

December 9
Light has come to continually shine
Changing forever eyes once blind
Light has come that guides the way
For seekers who seek night or day

Light has come to dwell within
The chambers deep where change begins
Light has come to be seen and known
Here and now on our journey Home

Thank You for Your glorious Light
That is my strength and song in the night
Thank You for Your Grace design
That is my solace rain or shine

By day the Lord directs His love,
at night His song is with me a prayer to the God of my life.
Psalm 42:8

December 10

Praise be to the God and Father of our Lord Jesus Christ, the
Father of compassion and the
God of all comfort, Who comforts us in all our troubles, so that we
can comfort those in any
trouble with the comfort we ourselves receive from God.
2 Corinthians 1:3-4

The "so that" is our purpose in pain
The reason that perseverance has its name
The comfort received is to be given away
To the soul that has had more than enough in one day

The "so that" encourages my heart today
Reminding me first of the One that gave His away
For all to know the exchange of comfort in the pain
For all to experience compassion that supernaturally sustains

Then sings my soul when my lips cannot
Then hear my prayer where my cries don't stop
Then know my need as none other can
Then comfort my heart to find rest in Your Hands

"So that" others may see and hear
Your Heart that is continually near
To be the Answer they too seek to know
To find Rest in You within their soul

God, make a fresh start in me, shape a Genesis week from the
chaos of my life.
Psalm 51:10 MSG

December 11
Hear ye
Come ye
Simply
Wholly

Hear ye
Come ye
Seeking
Wholly

Hear ye
Come ye
Finding
Wholly

You will seek Me and find Me when you seek Me with all your heart.
Jeremiah 29:13

O come let us adore Him
Christ the Lord…
-John Francis Wade, 1751

December 12
You are the God that gives
Every breath needed to live
You are the God that restores
Every heart to become fully Yours

You are the God that calms
Every soul with Your Song
You are the God that provides
Every need known inside

You are the God that spoke
Every Word of endless Hope
You are the God that speaks
Every moment instilling Peace

You are the God that redeems
Every heartache with Your dreams
You are the God that renews
Every endeavor to glorify You

In the beginning God…
Genesis 1:1

December 13
In the stillness of intentional time
Is the interactive Heart that touches mine
In the quietness of settled Grace
Is the interactive nearness of His embrace

In the peacefulness of surrendered will
Is the interactive Rest that He instills
In the soundlessness of hearing within
Is the interactive faithfulness without end

In the waiting before moving ahead
Is the interactive dependence of being Shepherd led
In the trusting of His reliable Hand
Is the interactive working of His sovereign plan

He has made everything beautiful in His time.
He has also set eternity in the human heart;
yet no one can fathom what God has done from beginning to end.
Ecclesiastes 3:11

December 14

The perfect Lamb of sacrifice
Paid the greatest debt for life
Trading Himself to save each of us
Through surrender in faithfulness

How amazing His Kingdom come
How Grace-filled His Will be done
How selfless the King for the crown-less ones
How priceless this Gift wrapped for everyone

The perfect Lamb of sacrifice
Paid the greatest debt for life
Trading Himself for each of us
Through surrender in faithfulness

No greater prayer to pray
No greater words to form and say
Than "Thy Kingdom come"
"Thy Will be done…"

God made Him Who had no sin to be sin for us,
so that in Him we might become the righteousness of God.
2 Corinthians 5:21

December 15
There is this quieted exchange
Of Grace just like the falling rain
Complete in a purposed thorough touch
Softening dry ground into sacredness

There is this most gentle provision
Of Grace given as His faithful decision
Decided before rain was even needed
Before a breath was given in Eden

There is this beauty above and beyond
Of Grace and Hope to rest upon
The surety alone of life heartfelt
Given as the priceless gift of Himself

For God so loved that world that He gave…
John 3:16

December 16

Timeless You are and shall always be
Timeless yet personal beyond degree
Timeless in the past and future yet present
Timeless Heart of the coming Advent

Timeless before the first word was spoken
Timeless through all that would be and is broken
Timeless yet permanent Hope within
Timeless eternally without end

Timeless precision in each step
Timeless decision for each breath
Timeless You continuously provide
Timeless You graciously abide

Your Word, Lord, is eternal; it stands firm in the heavens.
Your faithfulness continues through all generations;
You established the earth, and it endures.
Your laws endure to this day, for all things serve You.
Psalm 119:89-91

December 17
*Give thanks to the Lord for He is good.
His love endures forever.
Psalm 135:1*

Though there are impossible moments to breathe through
His love endures forever
Though there is heartache as the current view
His love endures forever

Though there is a mountain faced
His love endures forever
Though the word impossible seems the pace
His love endures forever

Though the days are long and nights longer
His love endures forever
Though the heart feels nothing but weak not stronger
His love endures forever

Though the motions are the only movement somehow
His love endures forever
Though the plan unfolding is the continued now
His love endures forever

Though the ache inside is great
His love endures forever
Though the heart feels lack to celebrate
His love endures forever

ON MY WAY HOME

The Lord is good, a refuge in times of trouble.
He cares for those who trust in Him.
Nahum 1:7

O soul are you weary and troubled?
No light in the darkness you see
There's light for a look at the Savior,
and life more abundant and free.
Turn your eyes upon Jesus,
look full in His wonderful face,
and the things of earth will grow strangely dim
in the light of His glory and grace.
-Helen H. Lemmel, 1922

December 18

There are so many needs and You meet each one
Through the Grace of your Kingdom come
Nothing impossible stands in Your way
Your Grace is unhindered like the sunrise each day

There are so many waiting for answers You'll show
Through the Grace given for all to know
Nothing but hesitation stands in the way
Of Grace already in place to be given each day

There are countless teachable moments You teach
Through Your Grace provided for each
There is Hope eternal and awaiting Peace
Of Grace prepared for surrendered feet

Show me Your ways, O Lord; teach me Your paths.
Lead me in Your truth and teach me,
for You are the God of my salvation;
on You I wait all the day.
Psalm 25:4-5 NKJV

Come and behold Him,
born the King of angels…
O come…
-John Francis Wade, 1743

December 19

You bring order and Peace
As I lay all down at Your feet
You turn chaos into sweetest calm
As I recall Your comfort within each Psalm

You turn moments into motion
As I encounter Your faithful devotion
You bring quieted sacredness
As I rest in Your faithfulness

You provide guide and lead
As I pray through each need
You speak intentionally
As I listen vertically

*Let the peace of Christ rule in your hearts… And be thankful.
Let the message of Christ dwell among you richly
as you teach and admonish one another with all wisdom
through psalms, hymns, and songs from the Spirit,
singing to God with gratitude in your hearts.
Colossians 3:15-17*

December 20
Brave enough to trustingly dance
In the timing of His romance
Brave enough to trustingly see
The wonders of His possibilities

Brave enough to trustingly wait
In the timing His Heart coordinates
Brave enough to trustingly adhere
In the wonders His Heart brings near

Brave enough to trustingly go
In the timing His Heart bestows
Brave enough to trustingly believe
In the wonders where His footprints lead

Brave enough to trustingly rest
In the timing of His steadfastness
Brave enough to trustingly abide
In the wonders His Heart provides

*How precious to me are Your thoughts
O God! How vast is the sum of them.
Psalm 139:17*

And wonders of His love...
- Isaac Watts, 1719

December 21
The shortest day holds the longest night
But never without Your inextinguishable Light
The season of winter that melts into spring
Brings the miracle of life again whispering

Do you hear the sound the heavens hold
Glory to God fear not but behold
Hope has come that fulfilled the dream
Of the final song of the Messiah King

No more night there but only day
Will be the Treasure without delay
When the trumpet loudly begins to play
The tune of redemption the King's on His way

*Did I not tell you that if you believed,
you would see the glory of God?
John 11:40*

December 22

Sometimes a walk is needed down memory lane
To honor in gratefulness Grace-bought change
The only rescue from ourselves
Is the abiding Peace of Emmanuel

Sometimes a leaf weighted down with wet rain
Is the best example of tears unexplained
The once was newness held in place
Was also held through Autumn's pace

There are no moments that separate
The ceaseless flow of Love never late
For He knows the before during and afterward
Through steadfast humility as Healing Lord

Mistakenly I misinterpreted pain
And ran like Jonah just the same
Thinking further away would bring needed change
But eventually found my longing rearranged

ON MY WAY HOME

You knew the time needed to grieve
You held me through my deepest need
You knew the tenderness I needed to feel
You held me through until I was still

How patient and loving Your endless ways
How tender Your Heart that holds mine each day
How loving in waiting to bring healing within
How faithful to be my Strength without end

*...nor height, nor depth, nor any other created thing
will be able to separate us from the
[unlimited] love of God,
which is in Christ Jesus our Lord.
Romans 8:39 AMP*

December 23

Perennials remember where they belong
Appointed moments to hear their song
Created for them perfectly timed
To display their dance lovingly designed

Perennials know when to rest
Appointed moments they don't contest
Trusting the depths not shallowness
Awaiting the display of faithfulness

Perennials come at just the right time
Created for display by design
To show the Story that has no end
Rooted in Glory resurrected again

Come to Me,
all you who are weary and burdened,
and I will give you rest.
Take My yoke upon you and learn from Me,
for I am gentle and humble in heart,
and you will find rest for your souls.
Matthew 11;28-29

December 24
May the soil of my heart meet Your soaking rain
In a quieted hush given that remains
Thoroughly until the depths within know
The hallowedness that stillness bestows

May the sacredness be my soul's desire
Receiving Your Word that wholly inspires
Lighting the path before me placed
In Your unending Fount of Mercy and Grace

For every day without fail
Is Your Love given come to dwell
Deep within the way You give
Teaching my heart to sing and live

How my soul receives again
Lovingkindness in place of my sin
Giving joy that rises in song
Resting in Whom my heart belongs

Let the morning bring me word of Your unfailing love,
for I have put my trust in You.
Show me the way I should go, for to You I lift up my soul.
Psalm 143:8

Jesus loves me this I know,
for the Bible tells me so…
-Anna B. Warner, 1859

December 25
Hallelujah what a Savior
Came to give us life forever
Hallelujah Christ has come
Came to be God's Will be done

Hallelujah through the night
Came to give unending Light
Hallelujah Shepherd led
Come to be our daily Bread

Hallelujah eternal Hope
Came to give what prophets spoke
Hallelujah praise angelically heard
Came to be the Living Word

*But when the kindness and
the love of God our Savior toward man appeared,
not by works of righteousness which we have done,
but according to His mercy
He saved us, through the washing of regeneration
and renewing of the Holy Spirit,
Whom He poured out on us abundantly
through Jesus Christ our Savior, that having
been justified by His Grace we should become heirs
according to the hope of eternal life.
Titus 3:4-7 NKJV*

Come and worship, come and worship
Worship Christ the newborn King
-James Montgomery, 1816

December 26

Christmas and Easter blessings have no end
Each holds the promise of the Beginning and Amen
Joy was held in Bethlehem's trough
Peace was held on Calvary's Cross

Love begat both calendar days
To bring Redemption over sin and the grave
Christmas began what Easter completed
Eden's curse was forever defeated

Christmas joy Easter provides
Both began eternity's Rest inside
So from now on we joyfully await
Anticipating His Return our Wedding date

From You comes the theme of my praise…
Psalm 22:25

And if I go and prepare a place for you,
I will come back and take you to be with Me
that you also may be where I am.
John 14:3

December 27

Praise the Lord. Praise the Lord, my soul.
I will praise the Lord all my life;
I will sing praise to my God as long as I live.
Psalm 146:1-2

This was the ordained day
Appointed for you to go away
To have your last breath here
And your next into eternity's cheer

The road led Home
By Grace and Mercy known
The road led Home
To see forever His Throne

This was the day you were welcomed Home
Into the final rest fully known
Through the Grace of Jesus bought and owned
To continue worshiping His Heart alone

The road led Home
Now visible Hope forever shown
The road led Home
To know forever His Shalom
(Miss you, Daddy…)

December 28
Love wrote the Story that began
Chapter and verse intentional by His Hand
Knowing precisely what would take place
And how quickly the Story would need His Grace

Oh the moment perfection was spoken
Oh the moment perfection was broken
Oh the moment His promise was made
Oh the heartache His mercy forgave

Now as each day begins anew
In His Story see this view
New mercies unendingly set in place
Within His Gift of redeeming Grace

*Blessed are those who have learned to acclaim You,
who walk in the light of Your Presence, O Lord.
Psalm 89:15*

Morning by morning new mercies I see;
all I have needed Thy HAND hath provided:
Great is Thy Faithfulness, Lord, unto me!
-Thomas O. Chisholm, 1923

December 29
Breath of Heaven still holds us together
Through every storm thought impossible to weather
Breath of Heaven still holds us through
Through every moment thought impossible to do

Breath of Heaven still holds us close
Through every moment thought impossible…He knows
Breath of Heaven still holds us thoroughly
Through every moment thought impossible…reassuringly

So do not fear, for I am with you;
do not be dismayed, for I am your God.
I will strengthen you and help you;
I will uphold you with My righteous right hand.
Isaiah 41:10

December 30
May I listen rest and rely
As Your faithfulness is supplied
May I learn rest and know
As Your faithfulness unfolds

May I learn rest and breathe
As Your faithfulness leads
May I linger rest and kneel
As Your faithfulness is revealed

May I look rest and wait
As Your faithfulness is great
May I live rest and abide
As Your faithfulness presides

Remain in Me, and I will remain in you.
John 15:4

Come with Me by yourselves to a quiet place and get some rest.
Mark 6:31

Because Thy promise I believe
O Lamb of God, I come…
-Charlotte Elliott, 1835

December 31
Faithful the message and Story
Written from the highest heights of glory
Recorded for every heart to know
To captivate every single soul

Through the Song of endless Grace
In Unseen footprints set in place
Through ordained moments meant to find
The Treasure of Heaven as yours and mine

Oh the joy when the angels dance
As each heart finds the true romance
Of Love that outlasts this purposed time
With unending Mercy forgiveness designed…

We now have this light shining in our hearts,
but we ourselves are like
fragile clay jars containing this great treasure.
This makes it clear that our
great power is from God, not from ourselves.
2 Corinthians 4:7

Bonus Blessing #1
You are God…I am not
Teach my thoughts to heed roadblocks
Help me surrender once again
To not repeat where I've been

Line in the sand has been drawn
You are the Strength I lean upon
Help my heart to trustingly know
You have everything in complete control

All not just parts or slivers
All is what Your Heart delivers
All of You for all of me
All the pieces I've yet to see

Trust in the Lord with all of your heart…
Proverbs 3:5

All to Jesus I surrender,
All to Him I freely give…
-Judson W. Van De Venter, 1896

Bonus Blessing #2
You have given Mercy and ask me to be merciful
You have given Grace and ask me to be gracious
You have given Love and ask me to be loving
You have given Willingly and ask me to be willing

You have given Peace and ask me to be peaceful
You have given Intentionally and ask me to be intentional
You have given Rest and ask me to be restful
You have given Joy and ask me to be joyful

You have given Faith and ask me to be faithful
You have given Generously and ask me to be generous
You have given Softly and ask me to be softened
You have given Breath and ask me to breathe…

*We give thanks for You, O God, we give thanks,
for Your Name is near; men tell of Your wonderful deeds.
Psalm 75:1*

Bonus Blessing #3
You're there in my struggles like morning dew
Provisional Mercies there to renew
You're there in the quiet amidst the chaos
Provisional Faithfulness through the Cross

You're there in every step given to take
Provisional Breath to walk by faith
You're there in the loudness of every stress
Provisional Peace encompassing Rest

You're there in my sadness and my grief
Provisional Solace giving new strength
You're there in my rhythm out of step
Provisional Staff that redirects

You're there in my prayerful tears
Provisional Nearness quieting fears
You're there in my greatest need powerfully
Provisional Grace through Calvary

In your distress you called and I rescued you, I answered you…
Psalm 81:7

I must tell Jesus all of my trials;
I cannot bear these burdens alone;
In my distress He kindly will help me;
He ever loves and cares for His own.
-E. A. Hoffman, 1894

Bonus Blessing #4

The already knowing each by name
The already knowing Your power of change
The already knowing every heartache and pain
The already knowing Your Hope that sustains

The already coming to abide
The already coming as Bread multiplied
The already coming selflessly decided
The already coming as Grace You provided

The already working together for good
The already working in what's not understood
The already working perfectly timed
The already working to wholly refine

The already interceding for each to hear
The already interceding You're forever near
The already interceding to seek then find
The already interceding for all to be Thine

*Out of His fullness we have all received
grace in place of grace already given.
John 1:16*

Bonus Blessing #5
Whatever this is I know You are greater than
And that You are holding me within Your anointed plan
That there is not a single breath that I take
That You did not first provide and make

Thank You that waiting has been never alone
That You placed others beside AND before Your Throne
Thank You for the answers You already know
And for Your perfect timing that is never slow

I lift up my eyes to the hills where does my Help come from?
My Help comes from the Lord, the Maker of Heaven and earth.
Psalm 121:1-2

Help is the gift You willing give
Help is strengthening to breathe and live
Help is aid in daily ordinary steps
Help is reviving in moments met

Help is the gift through daily Bread
Help is how You assist with the road ahead
Help is a nourishing in real time
Help is Your Hand that forever holds mine

…looking unto Jesus, the Author and Finisher of our faith…
Hebrews 12:2

I must tell Jesus all of my trials, I cannot bear my burdens alone
In my distress He kindly will help me,
He ever loves and cares for His own
I must tell Jesus! Jesus can help me, Jesus alone.
-E. A. Hoffman, 1894

Bonus Blessing #6

Change is not something in your pocket with a sound
Change is what God gives when Grace is found
Change is not from clothes you outwardly wear
Change is what Jesus gives when Grace is there

Change is not from your attitude that will not bend
Change is what the Spirit gives when Grace is within
Change is not from moving on undetected
Change is what Eternity gives when Grace is accepted

His divine power has given us everything we need for a godly life through our knowledge of Him who called us by His own glory and goodness.
2 Peter 1:3

About the Author

Each morning dawns in whispered
beauty spoken from His Heart to hers.
Being rooted in His Word daily has
deepened her walk with the Lord, and
has unexpectedly become her ministry.
That ministry being the gift of
encouraging others in what she has heard
on her way home…

Jane Spears has authored On My Way Home through her daily encounters with her Lord. She is a devoted wife of forty-four years, mother of two beloved daughters and grandmother, known as their Emmy. She especially enjoys her quiet morning walks, spending time with her family and delighting them with her baking.

Made in the USA
Columbia, SC
20 October 2024

44768380R00248